THE Bible

THE Bible

APPLYING GOD'S WORD TO YOUR LIFE

CHARLES R. SWINDOLL

with study helps by Val Harvey

BROADMAN PRESS
NASHVILLE, TENNESSEE

4261-32

ISBN: 0-8054-6132-9

Dewey Decimal Classification: 220

Subject Heading: BIBLE

Printed in the United States of America

Scripture quotations, unless otherwise marked, are from the *New American Standard Bible.* © The Lockman Foundation 1960, 1962, 1963, 1971, 1972, 1973, 1975, 1977. Used by permission.

Scripture references marked NIV are from the Holy Bible, *New International Version,* copyright © 1973, 1978, 1984 by International Bible Society.

Scripture verses marked TLB are taken from *The Living Bible.* Copyright © Tyndale House Publishers, Wheaton, Illinois, 1971. Used by permission.

Scripture references marked AMP are from *The Amplified Bible,* Old Testament. Copyright ©1962, 1964 by Zondervan Publishing House. Used by Permission. *The Amplified New Testament* ©The Lockman Foundation 1954, 1958, 1987. Used by permission.

Scripture references marked GNB are from the *Good News Bible,* the Bible in Today's English Version. Old Testament: Copyright © American Bible Society 1976; New Testament; Copyright © American Bible Society 1966, 1971, 1976. Used by permission.

Scripture references marked Phillips are reprinted with permission of Macmillan Publishing Co., Inc. from J. B. Phillips: *The New Testament in Modern English,* Revised Edition. © J. B. Phillips 1958, 1960, 1972.

Scripture references marked KJV are from the *King James Version* of the Bible.

Scripture references marked MLB are from *The Modern Language Bible, The New Berkeley Version.* Copyright 1945, 1959 © 1969 by Zondervan Publishing House. Used by permission.

This volume is affectionately
dedicated to four faithful men:

_____

Cyril Barber

Bill Butterworth

David Lien

Bill Watkins

_____

who serve behind the scenes at Insight
for Living, giving counsel and
encouragement to those who hurt,
finding in Scripture the foundation of
their faith. I am indebted to each man
for his unswerving commitment to
God's truth, his unselfish ministry to
people in need, his unceasing
discipline to stay at an endless task,
and his unsurpassed loyalty to my wife
and me as friends.

Contents

Introduction

For years I have wanted to write on doctrine . . . Bible doctrine. My flesh has been willing, but my spirit has been weak. That calls for an explanation.

The need for knowledge of the Scripture is obvious. Everywhere I turn I meet or hear about well-meaning Christians who are long on zeal but short on facts . . . lots of enthusiasm and motivation but foggy when it comes to scriptural truth.

They have a deep and genuine desire to be used by God, to reach the lost, to serve in the church, to invest their energies in "the kingdom of God and His righteousness," but their doctrinal foundation is shifting sand rather than solid rock. The result is predictable: They are at the mercy of their emotions, flying high one day and scraping the bottom the next. A frustrating yo-yo syndrome.

I know. For more years than I care to remember, I, too, climbed and tumbled, soared, and submerged, thought I knew the scoop, then later discovered how off-target I really was. The whole miserable mess leaves a person filled with doubt and disillusionment, grossly lacking in confidence, not to mention having that awful feeling of being exposed. At that point, most Christians decide to pack it in lest they get caught again in a similar position of vulnerability. You and I may be amazed to know how many have retreated into the background scenery of passivity simply because their ignorance of the basic building blocks caused them embarrassment.

Like I said, the need is obvious. Being a fixer-upper type, I am prompted to jump in with both feet and crank out a pile of pages that will provide the doctrinal ammunition so many Christians need. That's why I said my flesh is willing. But since I am also a let's-be-realistic type, I am reluctant.

Among the last things believers need is another dull volume on doctrine. Sterile and unapplied theology interests no one living in the real world. Most of those books wind up as great (and expensive!) doorstops. They also make a good impression when the pastor drops by for a visit and sees them lying there, freshly dusted, on the coffee table. And there is nothing like wading through thick theological works late at night to cure your battle with insomnia. Who hasn't come close to fracturing his nose on an eight-pound volume while trying to make it past page 3 in the prone position?

That's why my spirit is weak. Deep within me has been this growing fear of just pumping out another thick, boring book on doctrine that looks good but reads bad.

Theology Needs to Be Interesting

Since I am committed to accuracy, clarity, and practicality, I loathe the thought of publishing something that is anything but interesting, easily understood, creative—and yes, even captivating. See why my desire to write a book on doctrine has been on the back burner so long? It isn't easy to communicate the deepest truths of the Bible in an interesting manner. It has taken years for me to be convinced that it can be done . . . and even more years to be convinced that I may be able to do it. The chapters that follow are my best effort at accomplishing this objective. Only time will tell whether I have achieved my desire.

If my stuff makes sense, if the average individual is able to follow my thinking, picture the scenes, grasp my logic, come to similar conclusions, and later pass on a few of those thoughts to someone else, then the book will have made the impact I desired. But if it lacks real substance, or if the reader discovers it requires a graduate degree to track my thoughts, or even if it proves to be true to the biblical text yet comes across as tedious and pedantic, then my face, I can assure you, will be as red as your nose.

Introduction

The Need to Improve Theology's Reputation

Frankly, theology has gotten a bum rap. Just ask around. Make up a few questions and try them on for size in your church. You'll see. Many folks, if they are candid with you, will confess a distaste for sound biblical doctrines. Sound theology, like Rodney Dangerfield, "don't get no respect." You question that? Then let me suggest you do your own personal survey among some Christians. Ask things like:

- Ever made a study of the doctrines in the Bible?
- How would you respond if your pastor announced plans to bring a series of pulpit messages on several "important theological subjects"?
- Do you believe that all Christians ought to know where they stand doctrinally, or is that more the business of the clergy?
- When you hear the word *theology*, do you have a mental image of something interesting and stimulating? Or do you honestly think, *Dull stuff . . . please don't bore me?*
- On a scale of one to ten (ten being most important), how high would you rate a knowledge of theology?
- Can you remember a doctrinal sermon—or one lesson on theology you were involved in—that you actually *enjoyed?*
- Choosing your preference, rearrange these topics in the order you consider most interesting and timely. Which interests you the most? The least? Give each a number from one to seven.

_____ a biographical look at a biblical character

_____ a verse-by-verse analysis of a book in the New Testament

_____ a serious study of biblical doctrines

_____ what God's Word teaches about the home and family

_____ moral, social, and ethical issues according to Scripture

_____ biblical principles for success and personal motivation

———— Proverbs made practical for today

Unless you are most unusual, the study of doctrine would be ranked toward the bottom, if not altogether in last place. Compared to success principles on the home and family, "a serious study of biblical doctrines" does not seem nearly as important or relevant to most evangelical congregations. Yet, believe it or not, at the very heart of all those other topics is a great deal of theology.

It is surprising for most Christians to hear that their doctrinal position determines their interpretation and application of Scripture—whether or not they have ever declared themselves doctrinally. What roots are to a tree, the doctrines are to the Christian. From them we draw our emotional stability, our mental food for growth, as well as our spiritual energy and perspective on life itself. By returning to our roots, we determine precisely where we stand. We equip ourselves for living the life God designed for us to live.

Why Is Doctrine Often So Dull?

If all this is true, then why does the mere mention of theology turn off so many people? Why are most churches full of people programmed to think that doctrine is a synonym for dullness and boredom?

At the risk of appearing ultracritical, I'll be frank with you. Much of the problem lies with theologians who have done a poor job of communicating their subject. No offense, theological scholars, but you are notorious for talking only to yourselves. The language you employ is clergy code-talk, woefully lacking in relevance and reality. The terms you use are in-house jargon, seldom broken down into manageable units for people who aren't clued in. You may be accurate and certainly sincere, but your world is like the television series of yesteryear, "One Step Beyond." Please understand that we love you and respect you. No one would dare to question your brilliance. We need your gifts in the body and we admire your ability to stay at the disciplines of your studies. We just don't understand you.

As a result, much of what you write is kept within those

cloistered chambers that intimidate people who haven't had the privilege of probing the heavenlies as you have. The majority feel a distance from you when you share your secrets. I realize that many of you wish this weren't so, but I suppose it comes with the territory.

In this book and the others in this study series, my hope is to build a bridge of theological understanding with the common man, the uninitiated individual, the person who has never been to seminary—and doesn't care to to go—but really does want to develop a solid network of doctrinal roots.

I'm interested in reaching the truck driver, the athlete, the waitress, the high school student, the person in the military service, the homemaker who has a houseful of kids at her feet, the business person whose world is practical, earthy, tough, and relentless . . . and a hundred other "types" who have the brains to absorb biblical truth but lack the time and patience to look up every sixth or seventh word in a dictionary.

I therefore make no apology for approaching various subjects in a different way than standard theologians. I want everyone who picks up this book to understand every word and grasp every principle, even if you don't agree with them. (To disagree with me is your privilege—I expect it. In fact, I invite it. But to misunderstand or to *fail* to understand what I'm getting at would be tragic.)

I freely confess that I want you to enjoy this journey . . . to find out that discovering doctrine and seeing its importance can encourage you like nothing else. I want us to laugh together, as well as think together, as we dig into *the Book*. It's been my observation for the past twenty-five years of ministry that there is no subject too deep for anyone to understand if the material is presented creatively and clearly, sparked periodically by humor, and accompanied by illustrations that let plenty of life in. All this is true of folks who really want to learn.

By the way, that brings up another reason doctrine is dull to some people. As I implied earlier, they have a built-in, long-standing *prejudice* against it. Somehow, they have convinced themselves that (a) they don't need to fuss around with heady stuff like that since they aren't doing "full-time ministry," or (b) even if they made a study of the doctrines, all that knowledge would be of little practical value. In subtle ways these two excuses tend to plug their ears and clog the learning process.

Without trying to perform an overkill, both of those excuses are totally erroneous. Because every Christian is "doing full-time ministry," being theologically informed and equipped could not be more important. And since when does a knowledge of important facts lack practical value? If I recall Jesus' words correctly, that which makes us free is knowing the truth. It's ignorance that binds us, not knowledge. Furthermore, we are left defenseless before the cults and other persuasive false teachers if we lack this solid network of doctrinal roots. As I stated earlier, it stabilizes us.

An Approach that Will Keep Things Interesting

Before we get underway, let me explain my plan of approach.

I have no intention of writing an exhaustive theological treatment on all the biblical doctrines. (If you happen to be a perfectionist, expecting every jot and tittle to be addressed in this volume or the others in this series, please read that sentence again.) My plan is to offer a broad-brush approach to most of the essential points of evangelical truth. If you find certain details are not covered to your satisfaction or if you observe that some subjects of interest to you are not even mentioned, just remember that is on purpose. I'm hoping to whet your appetite for a much more intense and thorough study *on your own* once you've begun to get excited about these essential areas. Who knows? Maybe one day *you'll* be the one who will write a more thorough and analytical work. Be my guest.

You'll also want to keep a Bible handy. I'll try to quote as many of the main verses and passages as possible. But there will be times that I will give an additional reference or two which you might want to look up right then. If you have the time, please do that. Before too long you will begin to feel much more at home in the Scriptures. And use a good study Bible rather than a loose paraphrase or a copy of just the New Testament.

There are a number of study tools that make the Bible and its people come to life for you. *Commentaries* explore books of the Bible and tell you what scholars have discovered about the writers of the books, the times in which they lived, and what the Scriptures mean. *Bible encyclopedias, dictionaries,* and *handbooks* contain information about the people, places, and events in the Bible. They often include drawings and pictures to help you put yourself in the first-century world. *Bible atlases* have maps that show how the Holy Land looked at various times throughout history. Atlases usually give background information about governments and geography. *Concordances* tell you where words appear in the Bible. Pick a word like *love*; look it up just like you would in a dictionary; and you'll find a list of verses in which *love* is used. If you're serious about Bible study, you'll want to stop by a bookstore and invest in a good Bible handbook, atlas, and concordance. You'll be surprised how much those resources will add to your study.

At the end of the first chapter of each part of this book you will note several thoughts I call "Root Issues." These are simply practical suggestions designed to help you keep the doctrines out of the realm of sterile theory and in touch with the real world. To get the most out of these, I'd recommend that you purchase a handy-sized spiral notebook—your personal "Root Issues Notebook"—to record your thoughts, observations, and responses. Each chapter concludes with study questions. "Extending Your Roots" helps you explore what we've been talking about. "Taproot" takes you even further in your study of each doctrine. Don't be afraid to write your answers in this book. It's yours—make it personal.

Ten Major Areas of Doctrine

Finally, the outline I want to follow will be interwoven in this series of five study guides. All the doctrines I want to cover will fall within these ten major categories:

- The Bible
- God the Father
- The Lord Jesus Christ
- The Holy Spirit
- The Depravity of Humanity

- Salvation
- The Return of Christ
- Resurrection
- The Body of Christ
- The Family of God

As I mentioned earlier, the list is purposely not exhaustive, but there is plenty here to get our roots firmly in place. In fact, the better-known historic creeds down through the ages have included these ten areas. While considering this recently, I decided to write my own doctrinal credo, a statement of my personal faith. What it may lack in theological sophistication I have tried to make up for in practical terminology.

As I return to the roots of my faith, I am encouraged to find the time-honored foundations firmly intact:

- I affirm my confidence in God's inerrant Word. I treasure its truths and I respect its reproofs.
- I acknowledge the Creator-God as my Heavenly Father, infinitely perfect, and intimately acquainted with all my ways.
- I claim Jesus Christ as my Lord—very God who came in human flesh—the object of my worship and the subject of my praise.
- I recognize the Holy Spirit as the third member of the Godhead, incessantly at work convicting, convincing, and comforting.
- I confess that Adam's fall into sin left humanity without the hope of heaven apart from a new birth, made possible by the Savior's death and bodily resurrection.
- I believe the offer of salvation is God's love-gift to all. Those who accept it by faith, apart from works, become new creatures in Christ.

- I anticipate my Lord's promised return, which could occur at any moment.
- I am convinced that all who have died will be brought back from beyond—believers to everlasting communion with God and unbelievers to everlasting separation from God.
- I know the Lord is continuing to enlarge His family, the universal body of Christ, over which He rules as Head.
- I am grateful to be a part of a local church which exists to proclaim God's truth, to administer the ordinances, to stimulate growth toward maturity, and to bring glory to God.

With confidence and joy, I declare this to be a statement of the essentials of my faith.

That's where I stand . . . sort of a preview of coming attractions. Now it's time for you to dig in and discover where you stand. With God's help I think you will find this study one of the most important and interesting projects you have ever undertaken. You may even get so "fanatical" about your faith that your whole perspective on life changes.

Come to think of it, that's exactly what Christianity is supposed to do . . . change our lives.

I wish to thank my long-term, splendid secretary as I have so many times before. Helen Peters has done it again. Without regard for her own needs and preferences, she has deciphered my hand scratching, typed and retyped my manuscript, verified my footnotes, corrected my spelling, and helped me meet my deadlines. "Thank you" seems hardly sufficient to declare the depth of my gratitude. I also want to thank Val Harvey for her excellent work in writing the study questions for each of the volumes in this series.

And now let's dig in. You have stumbled your way through shifting sand long enough. May these books on Bible doctrine give you just the help you need so that you can stand firmly and finally on a foundation that is solid as rock.

Charles R. Swindoll
Fullerton, California

Part
I

Doctrine

1 The Value of Knowing the Scoop

Josh Billings was a humorist in the nineteenth century. On one occasion he said, "It is better not to know so much than to know so many things that ain't so." Which I suppose could be paraphrased, "Whatever ya know oughta be so!"

Jaime O'Neill, on the other hand, is a teacher in the twentieth century. The man has taught for about fifteen years in community colleges and currently teaches in a college in the state of Washington. Over the years O'Neill has become increasingly concerned about the lack of knowledge among so many of his students. It's not that he was concerned about their lack of technical knowledge or complex facts, but that so many of the general "facts" they thought they knew just "ain't so."

One day he decided to do something about it. Hoping to demonstrate to his students just how lacking they were in the basics—not simply to expose or to take potshots at their ignorance, but to help them see that they had a problem and they could hide it no longer—he devised an eighty-six-question quiz on general knowledge. He gave it to his college English class.

There were twenty-six people in the classroom, ranging in age from eighteen to fifty-four, all of whom had completed at least one quarter of college work. Remember now, these eighty-six questions were not what you would call complex, technical, or tricky. They were simple facts about the world around them—facts about people, facts about geography, facts about life in general. Professor O'Neill was so startled by what he discovered that he recorded his findings and later wrote about them in *Newsweek* in an article entitled "No Allusions in the Classroom." Here's a sampling of what he found that "ain't so."

> Ralph Nader is a baseball player. Charles Darwin invented gravity. Christ was born in the 16th century. J. Edgar Hoover was a 19th century president. . . . "The Great Gatsby" was a magician in the 1930s. Franz Joseph Haydn was a songwriter who lived during the same decade. Sid Caesar was an early Roman emperor. Mark Twain invented the cotton gin. . . . Jefferson Davis played guitar for the Jefferson Airplane. Benito Mussolini was a Russian leader of the 18th century; Dwight D. Eisenhower came earlier, serving as a president during the 17th century. . . . Socrates [was an] American Indian chieftian.

He adds:

> My students were equally creative in their understanding of geography. They knew, for instance, that Managua is the capital of Vietnam, that Cape Town is in the United States, and that Beirut is in Germany. Bogotá, of course, is in Borneo (unless it is in China). Camp David is in Israel, and Stratford-on-Avon is in Grenada (or Gernada). Gdansk is in Ireland. Cologne is in the Virgin Islands. Mazatlán is in Switzerland. Belfast was variously located in Egypt, Germany, Belgium and Italy. Leningrad was transported to Jamaica; Montreal to Spain.
>
> And on and on it went. Most students answered incorrectly far more often than they answered correctly. Several of them meticulously wrote "I don't know" 86 times, or 80 times, or 62 times. . . .
>
> As I write this, the radio is broadcasting the news about the Walker family. Accused of spying for the Soviets, the Walkers, according to a U.S. attorney, will be the Rosenbergs of the '80s. One of my students thought Ethel Rosenberg was a singer from the 1930s. The rest of them didn't know.
>
> As we enter the postindustrial "information processing" age, what sort of information will be processed? . . .[1]

As I smiled, shook my head, and laughed my way through that article, I was suddenly seized with the realization that general knowledge is fast slipping from us. For many, many years Americans have been considered a people who are supposed to be fairly well educated. No longer can we make this assumption. This makes me nervous. I get a little fearful over the ignorance that sweeps our television-addicted generation—the attitude that if someone doesn't do it for me, I'm not interested . . . or if someone doesn't think for me, I am not desirous of learning for myself.

—Root Issues—

1. Picture in your mind a friend or relative who is younger in the faith than you—perhaps still wrestling with some of the basics of belief in Christ. Picture this individual experiencing a sudden tragedy or crushing disappointment—or perhaps an encounter with a deceptive false teacher. Your friend, really struggling, looks to you for help. Is your grip on Bible knowledge strong enough to help your friend cope? Could you point him or her in the right direction? As you begin this book pray, "Lord, for the sake of _____ , I commit myself to this study." Write that person's name on a piece of paper and use it for a bookmark. It will be a reminder that a return to your roots may help others who look to you, as much as it helps yourself.

2. Look at Deuteronomy 6:4-9. If you are a parent of young children, visualize each of the "teaching opportunities" mentioned in verse 7. How might some of these opportunities be captured for God in your home and in your schedule? Note that this verse speaks specifically of teaching your children "by the way." In those early biblical days there was a great deal of time to talk as people walked from place to place. How might this same principle translate into our fast-paced, freeway-driving culture? Write these ideas in your personal notebook.

3. First Timothy 4:6 speaks of being "constantly nourished on the words of the faith and . . . sound doctrine."

What can you change in your daily schedule that would make it easier to draw this kind of nourishment from God's Word? It may be a matter of eliminating time-wasters, or it may be simply a matter of substituting "the best" in place of "the good." Nail down your thoughts by writing them out in your notebook.

Extending Your Roots

Based on what you already know about the Bible, complete the test and grade yourself.

1. The message of the Bible is _____.
2. The Bible contains _____ books written by _____ authors.
3. The Bible is the inspired Word of God. What does that sentence mean?
4. What are the original languages of the Bible?

_____

5. The word *testament* means _____.
6. The Old Testament begins with _____; the New Testament begins with _____.
7. The books of Law were written primarily by _____.
8. To read about doctrines, see the _____.
9. Two books of poetry in the Old Testament are _____

_____

10. Name the books of the Old Testament.

11. A favorite love story is _____.
12. Parables are _____.
13. What four men tell the same story each in his own way? _____, _____, _____, and _____.
14. The word *gospel* means _____.
15. Who is the Gentile writer of two New Testament books?
16. Which New Testament book focuses on the work of the Holy Spirit?_____

17. Jesus said before His ascension, "You shall be my
_____" (Acts 1:8).
18. The apostle Paul wrote _____ of the twen-
ty-one Epistles.
19. The only book of prophecy in the New Testament
is:_____.
20. God promises, at the end of the age, a new
_____ and a new _____
(Rev. 21:1).

Give yourself ten points for each correct answer.

What can you do to improve your grade?

Answers

1. Jesus Christ
2. sixty-six
4. Greek, Hebrew, Aramic
5. covenant
6. God, Jesus
7. Moses
8. Epistles
9. Psalms, Job, Song of Solomon, Proverbs, or Ecclesiastes
11. Ruth
12. Earthly stories with a heavenly meaning
13. Matthew, Mark, Luke, John
14. good news
15. Luke
16. Acts
17. witnesses
18. thirteen
19. Revelation.

2 | Ignorance Is Not Bliss

I want to state openly and forcefully that ignorance is not bliss—that ignorance, even in the general, secular realm, is the breeding ground for fear and prejudice, leading ultimately to superstition and slavery. An uneducated country is a defenseless country at the mercy of an educated country. Although I study every week, after reading that *Newsweek* article I suddenly wanted to study harder. I love to read and do research, but I found myself wanting to drink deeper at the fountain of knowledge.

Before going one step further, let me address all of you who make your living in the world of education. I have found words of encouragement: *Press on—never quit!* And to you who are in the process of getting an education, I offer the same counsel: Press on. Never stop studying. Never stop reading. Never stop learning. Don't believe something just because someone says it. Find out for yourself!

I read recently that an education is nothing more than going from an unconscious to a conscious awareness of one's ignorance. There is so much to be discovered!

What is true in the realm of general knowledge is equally true in the realm of spiritual knowledge. Talk about knowing things that "ain't so," I am constantly amazed at the level of *biblical* ignorance in these Unites States. Aren't you? I was watching the presidential elections in 1984. A well-known news commentator wanted to make reference to the Old Testament Book of 2 Chronicles. His notes, no doubt, used the Roman numeral two (II). As he read the line from the script, he called it "eleven Chronicles." The man may be culturally suave and politically sophisticated, but he has no idea how many Chronicles there are! He didn't mean to sound foolish; he just could not hide the fact that he is ignorant of the Scriptures.

That's bad enough for a person who doesn't claim to be a Christian, but how about you?

What if someone gave you a piece of paper with eighty-six questions on it—just basic information about your faith? How would you do? Or what if someone came rapping at your door tomorrow morning and said, "I would like to talk with you about this wonderful class we have. We're meeting with some of your neighbors and we're studying the Bible together. We'd like you to attend the class with us." The more the two of you talk, the more you realize this person is not from your church and doesn't represent your faith. Later on, the same individual makes these comments, "Oh, I understand where you're coming from. You must really live under the delusion that Jesus is God. Do you realize . . . ?" And then he and his partner quote three or four verses that seem to contradict the Deity of Christ.

How would you do in that situation? Could you stand alone and convince them otherwise?

Or perhaps you've picked up a very convincing piece of literature that makes an attack against the Scriptures and says, in effect, "Really, it's the work of man. Those men who wrote the Scriptures were zealous and sincere but not actually 'inspired.' That which has been passed on to us really isn't that credible." As you read those words, could you convince yourself the information was unreliable? To do so requires knowing the scoop. Do you?

There is a great section of Scripture in the New Testament that contains some words of exhortation about our growing up as we learn and discover truth for ourselves.

> And who is there to harm you if you prove zealous for what is good? But even if you should suffer for the sake of righteousness, you are blessed. And do not fear their intimidation, and do not be troubled, but sanctify Christ as Lord in

your hearts, *always being ready to make a defense* to everyone who asks you to give an account for the hope that is in
you, yet with gentleness and reverence; and keep a good con-
science so that in the thing in which you are slandered, those
who revile your good behavior in Christ may be put to shame
(1 Pet. 3:13-16, emphasis mine).

The first-century recipients of Peter's Letter were hurt-
ing. They were suffering people. So Peter writes to encourage them, lest they become intimidated and fearful. That's
why, in the midst of this word of encouragement, he drops a
comment about their being able to "make a defense" of
their faith. And it isn't just a casual comment exclusively
reserved for ancient Christians. It is truth for all Christians
in every generation. It's a command.

Look closely at verse 15 once again:

But sanctify Christ as Lord in your hearts, always being
ready to make a defense to everyone who asks you to give an
account for the hope that is in you, yet with gentleness and
reverence.

The words "make a defense" come from the Greek term
apologia. We get our word *apologetic* or *apology* from it. Not
in the sense of apologizing or saying you're sorry for something. The idea of "apology" carries with it the thought of a
formal justification, a convincing defense. Let's use those
words: "Always being ready to make a formal justification
or to give a convincing defense to any one who asks." Not
only for our sakes, but for younger and less mature Christians who may not be able to defend themselves. God often
exhorts His people to have a good deal of biblical savvy.

Extending Your Roots

1. The apostle Paul had to "make a defense" of his faith
many times. Trace his court appearances in Acts 21—26.
List each scene and Paul's apology.

2. Because of Jewish opposition, would Paul ever have been freed?

 *Taproot*

You are on trial. You have been charged with being a follower of Jesus Christ. The following court scene will help you make a defense of your faith. See if you are guilty as charged.

SCENE: A court room
PRINCIPALS: Judge, attorney, court officer, witness, spectators
COURT OFFICER: Silence in the court! The session is about to begin.
JUDGE: Are all the officiating parties present?
COURT OFFICER: Yes, your honor.
JUDGE: Good. Who is the first case?
OFFICER: (*your name*), Your Honor. He wants to defend himself and the charge that he is a follower of Jesus.
YOU:

JUDGE: Have you ever doubted Him or your decision to follow Him?
YOU:

JUDGE: I suppose you believe that book . . . the Bible?

Growing Deep in the Christian Life: The Bible

YOU:

JUDGE: You say this book has revealed a life-style pleasing to God?
YOU:

JUDGE: Will the witness take the stand? Tell me, what kind of follower of Jesus is the defendant?
WITNESS:

(witness is dismissed)
JUDGE: If I were to ask other people who know you for a Christian character reference, what would they say?
YOU:

JUDGE: One more question. Is following Jesus a temporary choice for you?
YOU:

JUDGE: I find this defendant guilty as charged and sentence him to life as a Christian *or* I find this defendant not guilty! (*Underline the correct decision.*)

3 Knowing the Scoop Is Often Emphasized in Scripture

Let me take you on a brief scriptural safari. This journey will take us quickly through the Scriptures. In the ancient days under Moses, God was so concerned that His people know His truth that He, with His finger as it were, wrote His laws into stone. Moses brought the stone tablets down from a mountain in his arms. He presented them to the people and explained that these words were to be a guide for their lives. God wanted His people to know His truth.

Before the people marched into Canaan, Moses pulled the Israelites aside for a final review. The Book of Deuteronomy contains his sermons [*deutero*, "second"; *nomos*, "Law" or "a repetition of the Law"]. It is a book in which Moses repeats and applies the law as he delivers no less than seven sermons to the people of God. In the sixth chapter of Deuteronomy he tells the fathers and mothers to take the truth of God and instruct their children in it, because the children were soon to be exposed to a whole new life-style that would cut across the grain of their belief and faith in one God. They would soon be moving into a land characterized by idolatry and polygamy. They would be exposed to a whole new way of thinking. So Moses said ahead of time, "These children must *know* the truth. Teach them." Pause and read Deuteronomy 6 for yourself—great chapter!

As early as the days of Samuel, a school of the prophets had been established. Such a school was made up of a body of men who were interested in honing their skills and becoming spokesmen for God. They trained at the feet of

Samuel and other men of God. They became known as prophets of God who knew God's truths.

In the days of captivity, God's continual reproof to His people was, "You did not act upon what you knew. You acted in ignorance." They failed to apply the theology they had been taught, hence, they fell into captivity in a foreign land.

In the days of Jesus, how often our Lord looked at the scribes and Pharisees and rebuked them with the words, "Do you not *know*? Have you not *read*?" He said that to the clergy of His day. "Why are you ignorant of what the scrolls say?"

When Jesus departed from the earth, He left the church in the hands of the apostles. They wrote letters to both churches and individuals. The letters contain truth for us to read, to learn, to put to use, to pass on to others. Frequently, we find words like "know this" and "stand fast" and "I would not have you to be ignorant about" and "be ready to defend your faith" threaded through those letters. Throughout the Bible God's repeated command to the people of God is "learn, study, grow, equip your mind with My words so that you can defend your position when asked about it or when faced with attack."

I recently did a brief analysis of church history. As I surveyed the subject, I was encouraged and refreshed all over again by the lives of men and women who took the Book seriously and, when necessary, laid down their lives for it. Some of them wrote our creeds which exist today. Some of them gave us the dogma upon which we stand. They systematized our theology. Others gave us our hymns so that we could sing our faith. And, in fact, they wrote catechisms for the young so that children might be cultivated in a knowledge of the truth. Our own American heritage finds many of our principles rooted in the pages of Scripture. It wasn't uncommon for higher education to be interwoven with biblical truth.

Do you know how long it was that our forefathers stayed on this continent before they established a school of higher learning? A mere sixteen years. They survived those bitter winters. They built their houses. As early as possible they established their government. Some then devoted themselves to establishing an educational center in a little place called Newtown, which was later changed to Cambridge. And they named that school, the first American school of higher learning, after a thirty-one-year-old clergyman who had died prematurely. He had left his library and half his estate to the school. His name was John Harvard.

Ever read the cornerstone at Harvard University? When I ministered at Massachusetts, back in the mid 1960s, I remember driving down to that campus. During a harsh winter storm, I stood knee-deep in snow near the wall that contained the etched cornerstone. I wiped the ice and snow off the bronze plate and copied these words:

> After God had carried us safe to New England and wee had builded our houses, provided necessaries for our livelihood, reared convenient places for God's worship, and settled the civil government, one of the next things wee longed for and looked after was to advance learning and perpetuate to posterity, dreading to leave an illiterate ministry to the churches when our present ministers shall lie in the dust.

Think of it! The very first institution of higher learning was established to give to the colonies a literate ministry, a body of thinking, devoted, biblically committed believers who would stand in the gap, who would have a knowledge of the truth that was strong and firm and courageous against the attack of the enemy, for surely such attacks would come. How essential it is that we who claim to love the Lord and commit ourselves to the truth in His Word *know* where we stand!

 *Extending Your Roots*

1. Read Deuteronomy 6 and underline in your Bible the truths that help us relate the Word of God to our daily lives.

2. For additional study, compare the Scripture parallels in Exodus 12:24-27; 13:3-10; 11-16.

 *Taproot*

1. Think about the many doctrines in the Bible. Here are a few:

- The Bible
- God the Father
- The Lord Jesus Christ
- The Holy Spirit

2. Select one of the above doctrines or another preference. Using the Scripture, study, learn, grow, equip your mind with as many truths as you can find on the doctrine. List definite facts or instructions you can *know*. Refer to this assignment throughout the study of this book and continue adding more of "the scoop."

4 | Benefits of Being Spiritually Informed

Why is it so important to be well grounded in the truth of God? Why bother to know the scoop? Why not leave that responsibility to the missionary and minister? Let me suggest six specific reasons. There may be many more, but these six are essential. Each one is something we must personally enter into.

1. Knowledge gives substance to faith. On what do those who do not know the truth rely? On emotion, on feelings, on someone else's opinion, on a book, on tradition, or some other empty, humanistic hope. And the result? Their faith lacks substance. That is especially revealing when they are under attack or when testing comes. That thought introduces the next benefit.

2. Knowledge stabilizes us during times of testing. When we know what God has said, and then we go through a period of pain when the bottom virtually drops out of our life, we don't panic, we don't doubt, we don't ship the faith. The knowledge we have gained stabilizes us and equips us with essential, calming fortitude when the tests come.

3. Knowledge enables us to handle the Bible accurately. By knowing the general themes of Scripture, we are better able to handle the Scriptures intelligently and wisely. A working knowledge of the doctrines, for example, gives us confidence in using Scripture.

4. Knowledge equips us to detect and confront error. As I mentioned earlier, when you know where you stand spiritually, no one can get you off course. When you're hearing erroneous information, you don't need someone to nudge you and say, "Did you get that? Listen to that. That's not true, is it?" Or, "You know, in light of what Scripture teaches, what he just presented is out of whack." Why? Because you have gone to the trouble to know the scoop. You can't be intimidated. Your antennae have been sensitized.

5. It makes us confident in our daily walk. Show me a person who stumbles along in the Christian faith, and I'll show you a person who isn't exposing himself or herself to a consistent intake of the Scriptures. The learning process has somehow been stifled, interrupted, or put on "hold." Biblical knowledge and personal confidence are like Siamese twins, inseparably linked together.

6. A good foundation of spiritual truth filters out our fears and superstitions. How important! I think we would all be amazed if we knew how many people operated their lives from superstition and fear. God's truth has a way of silencing those erroneous voices that would otherwise siphon our inner energy and immobilize us.

Before proceeding any further, let's take the time to meditate on two passages of Scripture. I will quote the first from *The Modern Language Bible: The New Berkeley Version,* Hosea 4:1-6. The other will be a paraphrase from *The Living Bible*: Amos 8:11-13. Both are from minor prophets who had a major message for their times and ours as well.

> Listen to the word of the Lord, sons of Israel; for the Lord has a charge against the dwellers of the land, because there is no fidelity, no kindness, no knowledge of God in the land. There is swearing, lying, murder, theft, adultery, violent outbreaks, bloodshed after bloodshed. Wherefore the land mourns, and everything living in it languishes. . . .
>
> Even at that, let no one enter complaint; let no one bring accusation, for My people are like their priestlings. You priests! You stumble by day; the prophet, too, stumbles with you by night. . . . My people perish for lack of knowledge, and because you have rejected knowledge, I reject you from being priest to Me. Since you have forgotten the law of your God, I, too, will forget (Hos. 4:1-6, MLB).
>
> "The time is surely coming," says the Lord God, "when I

will send a famine on the land—not a famine of bread or water, but of hearing the words of the Lord. Men will wander
everywhere from sea to sea, seeking the Word of the Lord,
searching, running here and going there, but will not find it.
Beautiful girls and fine young men alike will grow faint and
weary, thirsting for the Word of God" (Amos 8:11-13, TLB).

Even though those two prophecies are many centuries
old, they slice through the fog of our times and speak with
incredible relevance today. Is there not a devastating famine in our land? Is there not a thirst for the unadulterated
truth of God?

Periodically, I am invited to speak to groups of people who
wish to know more of what God's Word teaches. I have, on
certain occasions, begun those sessions by saying, "I am
here today because there is a famine in the land—but not
the kind of famine sweeping across India or sections of Afri-
ca. This famine is in America and most other places on
earth. Not a famine of food or water . . . not a famine of
churches or religious ministries. This is a famine like the
ancient prophets mentioned—a famine of hearing the truth
of the Word of God." To support those statements, I will often read the prophecies from Hosea and Amos.

Invariably, heads begin to nod in agreement. After such
sessions I have interacted with people who respond to those
words by relating how starved they are for the life-giving,
encouraging, enlightening instruction of Scripture.

The teaching of biblical doctrine is as rare as it is valuable! Yet I'm not suggesting that such doctrinal knowledge
is an end in itself, but a means to an end. Those who hope to
survive with any measure of emotional sanity and mental
stability must have a solid diet of sound biblical theology,
clearly understood, consistently digested, regularly put into
action.

Extending Your Roots

1. Review the six reasons we should be spiritually informed:

(1) Knowledge gives substance to faith.
(2) Knowledge stabilizes us during times of testing.
(3) Knowledge enables us to handle the Bible accurately.
(4) Knowledge equips us to detect and confront error.
(5) Knowledge makes us confident in our daily walk.
(6) Knowledge filters out our fears and superstitions.

2. Now, read the following life situations and match them with the proper benefit of being spiritually informed. Place the appropriate number in the blanks provided.

_____ Larry and Patricia watched the doctors come and go as they waited with their neighbors in the emergency room. Jimmy had run out in front of a speeding car. The couple tried to silently think of Scripture verses to share with their grieving neighbors, something comforting from God. "Why can't I remember just one verse?" Probably because they were half-hearted hearers.

_____ Sue is a "church-hopper." Churches offering the most in programs and entertainment interest her. Too much changing membership has caused her to become uninvolved in Bible study. Recently Sue encountered opposition in the office where she works. A coworker falsely accused her of misusing office hours. Sue was innocent. She began sending "SOS" emergency prayers to God, who seemed not to care about the attack. It never occurred to Sue that something was wrong with her faith in God.

_____ Thelma has been a Christian for sixty years. And, yet, fear controls her life. Her children, grandchildren, the weather, war, and the church leadership are just a few of her worries. Somewhere in all those years of churchgoing, Thelma missed something.

_____ Jerri was taking a special-interest class at a nearby community college. Near Eastern religions had always fascinated her. Three nights a week she listened to a man lecture on various mystic religions. Jerri began to feel uneasy about his teachings. The focus of the lectures were contrary to the Bible. Dropping the class was the only solution for her.

_____ John, a healthy forty-year-old, was playing basketball at the church gym. Suddenly severe pains seared through his left arm and chest. "Dial 911" was the last thing he remembered hearing. Days later, in the intensive-care unit, John became alert, but his faith in God's watch care over him didn't. All those hours studying biblical history and now . . . .

_____ David is a "roller-coaster" Christian. Sometimes he's up. The uptimes happen when he is actively involved in Bible study and prayer; "the downs" occur when his weekends are overbooked with other things. However, one Sunday morning he heard a challenging sermon on the Christian's daily walk. David discovered a way to get off the "coaster."

Taproot

1. Survey the Book of Hosea or the Book of Amos. Read the entire book at one sitting. Begin making notes about the relevance of this book for today. Note that the major message of each prophet for his time is essentially the same for ours.

2. Conclude your survey with a written description of "a famine of hearing the truth of the Word of God."

5 | Sound Doctrine Is Invaluable

For the next few moments, let's consider some vital words written to a young pastor named Timothy. The Letter is 1 Timothy, chapter 4. This chapter, written to a minister at a local church in the city of Ephesus, contains special instructions on various subjects related to the ministry. The first six verses have to do with that which will occur in later times. Certainly, our own times would be included in that phrase, "in later times."

> But the Spirit explicitly says that in later times some will fall away from the faith, paying attention to deceitful spirits and doctrines of demons, by means of the hypocrisy of liars seared in their own conscience as with a branding iron, men who forbid marriage and advocate abstaining from foods, which God has created to be gratefully shared in by those who believe and know the truth. For everything created by God is good, and nothing is to be rejected, if it is received with gratitude; for it is sanctified by means of the word of God and prayer. In pointing out these things to the brethren, you will be a good servant of Christ Jesus, constantly nourished on the words of the faith and of the sound doctrine which you have been following (1 Tim. 4:1-6).

The writer (Paul) begins rather forcefully: "But the Spirit explicitly says. . . ." Before proceeding, pause long enough to understand the force of those five opening words, especially the term *explicitly*. Why would he add "explicitly"? Why wouldn't he just say, "the Spirit says," or "thus says the Lord"? Because "explicitly" adds emphasis to what is to follow. The term *explicitly* (and it's used only here in all the

New Testament) means "expressly, most assuredly in stated terms." It is introducing an unequivocal fact. Not merely a hunch or a pretty good idea that something will probably occur. No, this is absolutely reliable information.

I thought of that word "explicitly" while I was reading about earthquakes some time ago. While doing some research on those horrible experiences that our southern neighbors in Mexico City endured, I came across these lines:

> In this country, geologists say that a major earthquake not only can but will strike somewhere in California with appalling loss of life and enormous property damage. A quake of a magnitude greater than 8.0—. . . has a 50-50 chance of happening on the southern section of the San Andreas fault within the next 30 years, according to estimates prepared for the National Security Council. Estimates are that it will kill between 3,000 and 13,000 people, depending on the time of day [1]

Geologists, in the words of 1 Timothy 4, explicitly state that a major earthquake will hit California, which happens to be my place of residence! It isn't simply a theory. It isn't an exaggerated scare tactic based on some fanatic's hunch or a haunting idea; it is fact.

By the way, when I was reading that article, someone on the second floor of our home cranked up the vacuum cleaner. I will never forget that moment! I almost lost it when the very moment I read that frightening fact I began hearing noises and feeling vibrations. I experienced *explicit* panic!

The Spirit *explicitly* states that something is a fact—a fact that is even more sure than the prediction of a California earthquake. What? "That in later times some will fall away from the faith." The Greek term translated "fall away" is the same word we use in English—*apostasize*, "abandon, withdraw from, leave." In today's terms: "In later times, some will bail out theologically."

Why? Why would someone want to leave something as marvelous as the Christian faith? Why would anyone choose to defect in doctrine? We are told why: "Because they will begin to pay attention to deceitful spirits"—that's the *style* of teaching they'll get exposed to, "and doctrines of demons"—that's the *source* of such teaching. We don't like to call it that. In our devil-ignoring, demon-denying era, we're reluctant to suggest such radical thoughts (and nothing could delight our adversary more!), but Scripture clearly states that he is behind the scenes of spiritual apostasy. It is satanic in source. There will be doctrines that come from the pit, but they will be deceitfully displayed as truth—convincingly so.

How? Verse 2:

> by means of the hypocrisy of liars seared in their own conscience as with a branding iron.

False teachers have no qualms about leading people into the realm of error. They're convinced that what they are teaching is true. Along with an abundance of charisma, they have the ability to persuade others to buy into their position. And they have what they call "facts" to pull you away from where you stand. Again, this is not some superficial tactic from a wild-eyed fanatic— it is true. Remember the Spirit *explicitly* warns of such.

And to go a step further, Paul, the writer, mentions the teaching of one of the first-century heresies: gnosticism. Gnostics taught that matter was evil, and that whatever was physically pleasing to humans was spiritually displeasing to God—which would include things like marriage and eating certain foods. So they taught, "You're not to marry, and you shouldn't eat certain foods."

> men who forbid marriage and advocate abstaining from foods, which God has created to be gratefully shared in by those who believe and know the truth (v. 3).

Interestingly, we don't find the apostle Paul biting off his nails and churning within, wondering, "How do I respond to these things? Could they be true?"

He simply says, "But that's not true!"

How could Paul be so sure that what the Gnostics taught wasn't true?

> For everything created by God is good, and nothing is to be rejected, if it is received with gratitude; for it is sanctified by means of the word of God and prayer (vv. 4-5).

He was confident and calm in the face of heresy because he knew the theological scoop. In fact, he gives wise, needed counsel to all who are ministers of the gospel. In verse 6 he says: "In pointing out these things to the brethren, you will be a good servant of Christ Jesus."

In other words, Timothy, here's how you're to spend much of your time: "constantly nourished on the words of the faith and of the sound doctrine which you have been following."

Isn't that helpful? That one statement gives ministers (especially pastors) a large part of their job description. We are responsible for nourishing ourselves in the Book consistently and faithfully. And the longer we are in ministry, the more we *need* to be nourished because the greater the pressure, the more the problems, the more the temptations, the more the calendar will get filled with other things.

Today I could not be more thankful for the doctrinally sound graduate school where I studied, for mentors who loved the truth and helped me understand it, for parents who taught me the way, for a wife who helped put me through the earlier years of my higher education, for congregations who patiently prayed, believed, and encouraged me as I forged out my theology right up to this present moment. I am grateful for so many who had a hand in my learning, growing experience. By the way, it is still going on!

My question to you is this: Where are *you* in the learning process? Are you learning your way through God's Book? Is doctrine important to you? Or do you think of it as dull, irrelevant stuff? Hopefully, by the time you've worked your way through this book, you will be more convinced than ever that doctrine—rather than being dull—is downright essential and exciting. We must never stop learning and growing in our faith!

Let me make it even more practical. Would you ever think of going to a physician who had decided to stop studying? I doubt it. I don't think anyone would ever say to his wife who was in need of medical help, "Just check the yellow pages, Honey. Any one of those guys with 'M.D.' after his name is fine." Never! We select only the ones we respect. And even then, we may get a second and sometimes a third opinion. Why? We want to know if the physician diagnosing our ailment is still growing, if he or she is still learning, still practicing good medicine. The same could be said for an attorney who takes our complicated case and defends us before a court of law. Because we are at the mercy of the person's intelligence, integrity, and knowledge of law, we want to be certain of his or her practice.

One of my major objectives in this book and the other books in the *Growing Deep* series is to help equip you to stand firm amidst the strong and subtle currents of our day. In Paul's words, to explain "the words of the faith" and to offer reliable instruction in "sound doctrine" (v. 6). I'll do my best to keep it interesting and clear if you will do your best to concentrate—mentally devoting yourself to each subject.

But just at this very point, a warning is in order. An intellectual knowledge of doctrine—by itself—can be dangerous.

Extending Your Roots

1. A topical study means selecting a particular topic and locating and comparing all the verses you can find on the subject. Conclude the study with a comparison of the related words and your observations.

Topic: Unsound Doctrine

Word list:

- false teachers
- apostasy
- Gnostics
- heresy

Resources: A *concordance* is a word index. Principal words of the Bible are listed alphabetically, then book, chapter, and verse references in the Bible are given.

A *topical Bible* lists Scriptures by topics.

2. What are some unsound doctrines in our world today?

One of the major purposes of the Book of Jude was to remind the church about heresy. The church had been repeatedly threatened by false teaching.

Outline the book looking for ways to defend God's truth.

I.

II.

6 Knowledge Alone Can Be Dangerous

As I conclude this part of our study, I should warn us against some of the dangers of knowledge. I can think of at least four:

1. Knowledge can be dangerous when it lacks scriptural support—intelligent, biblical support. Knowledge just for knowledge's sake is a heady thing and can turn into pride. God's Word frequently warns us about being full of knowledge and feeling "puffed up" because of it.

2. Knowledge can be dangerous when it becomes an end in itself. God gave us His truth so that we may put it into practice, not simply store it up.

3. Knowledge can be dangerous when it isn't balanced by love and grace. Such knowledge results in arrogance, which leads to an intolerant spirit . . . an exclusive mind-set.

Ever been around a group of people who think they've got a corner on the truth? I call this "the Bible club" mentality. And because you're not in it, you're out to lunch and they're cool. That's a dangerous thing. When knowledge leads to an intolerance of other people, it has gone beyond proper bounds. Knowledge that isn't balanced with love and grace is truth gone to seed.

4. Knowledge can be dangerous when it remains theoretical—when it isn't mixed with discernment and action. More on that in the next section.

Now, I know there are some who are thinking, "Hey, Chuck, give me a break, man. I'm getting up in years. I've paid my dues. You minister-types can get all excited about that truth, but it's enough to know I'm saved. I'm not going to hell. I know I'm gonna be with Jesus when I die. Just don't make me think. I'm tired. Just tell me, and I'll believe it."

Do you know the problem with that kind of response, my friend? It's that you've forgotten that you have people around you who respect you and need you to stand firm. They look up to you. And they rely on you to know. You may not like to read this, but in some ways you're their theological defense. They *need* you to know the scoop.

I love the way C. S. Lewis put it:

> If all the world were Christian it might not matter if all the world were uneducated. But, as it is, a cultural life will exist outside the church whether it exists inside or not. To be ignorant and simple now—not to be able to meet the enemies on their own ground—would be to throw down our weapons, and to betray our uneducated brethren who have, under God, no defense but us against the intellectual attacks of the heathen.

Then he concludes:

> Good philosophy must exist, if for no other reason, because bad philosophy needs to be answered. The cool intellect must work not only against cool intellect on the other side, but against the muddy heathen mysticisms which deny intellect altogether. Most of all, perhaps, we need intimate knowledge of the past . . . the learned life then is, for some, a duty.[1]

Our problem is not that we know so many things, it's that we know so much that just "ain't so." My hope is that this book will help clear that out of the way so we can find out what *is* so.

For most of us that's more than a nice idea. It's a duty.

 *Extending Your Roots*

1. Evaluate where you are in the learning process by ranking yourself from 1 to 10. The number 1 is a low level of learning and 10 is the highest level.

_____ Studying the Bible
_____ Understanding sound doctrines
_____ Learning to meditate and pray
_____ Drawing strength from God's Word

2. List things you can do to improve low levels of learning.

 ── *Taproot* ──

1. Purchase a book on biblical doctrines and begin reading a chapter each week to help in your learning process.

2. Write an explanation for each of the "ifs."
Knowledge alone can be dangerous if:
- scriptural support is lacking
- it becomes an end in itself
- it isn't balanced with love and grace

Discernment

7 Don't Forget to Add a Cup of Discernment

For many people life is two-dimensional—rather plain and drab. It lacks depth and color. Like staring at a blank wall.

There was a period of time in my life when that was true. During that time the most important thing to me was simply the gaining of knowledge. It's not that there was something wrong with that. It's just that something terribly important was missing during that period of my life. My interest was strictly in getting hold of biblical facts . . . gaining a thorough knowledge of scriptural doctrines. I wanted to know what God's Book was all about. I wanted to understand how it fit together. In my pursuit of knowledge, I diligently probed the Bible much like Sergeant Friday in the old "Dragnet" television show. I wanted the facts, "just gimme the facts."

Thanks to the teaching of a very persuasive and powerful minister whose stated desire was to communicate the doctrines of the Bible, I became virtually brainwashed with his approach and system of thinking. And all who sat under his ministry for very long had the same mind-bending experience. A knowledge of doctrine became our watchword. Everyone outside our circle was judged on the basis of how much they knew. And since they never seemed to know as much as we did, we looked down our noses at them! I don't believe I was ever more legalistic than during those years, even though all of us in the group would never have admitted such a thing. I mean, legalism was something other people demonstrated, not us.

I absorbed an enormous amount of information, some of which I came to realize later was spurious. But I did begin to grasp a measure of truth, and that was stimulating to me because I was so blatantly ignorant of how the Scriptures fit together. As I look back and reflect on those days, I must confess I grew, not only in knowledge, but every bit as much in pride . . . a pride so hideous it was like a growing cancer in my life. What I gained in knowledge I lacked in compassion and care for others. There was a lack of tolerance for people who would not agree with my system of thought. Other Christians became increasingly less important to me. In addition, non-Christians were virtually outside the scope of my inner radar screen.

While I was growing in biblical facts, I was diminishing in what we might call the third dimension of life; color, depth of character, a broader appreciation for the whole of living. My joy was conspicuous by its absence as I became more demanding, more rigid. And I'm not the rigid type! I became more structured. And I am not much of a structured person in my personality. Furthermore, very little creativity flowed through my mind. My world was reduced to a spectrum of blacks and whites and a very few grays. No color. No beauty. No cushion. No room for people who happened to disagree. Not much laughter and, most unfortunately, not much love. God became a lifeless Deity to be studied, a sterile caricature put together in an outline of theological topics, well systematized and perfectly memorized.

Looking back on all that, what I gained was intellectual knowledge and what I lacked was wise discernment. And rather than cultivating an open mind to new truth and open arms for new people, I pushed them away. I realize now, with much regret, that I became a blind slave to a system of thought rather than a discerning servant of the living God, committed not only to His principles but also to His people.

I had grown in knowledge, but not in grace.

Now, why do I unload all this? Because I want to save you from the same pitfall. And because I want you to remember all the way through our study of doctrine that these truths are to enhance our walk with God and our relationship with others, not *hinder* it. To borrow from Solomon, let's learn wisdom and understanding along with biblical facts. Let's learn a fear of the Lord as well as the Word of the Lord.

Please don't misunderstand. It's OK to deal with facts. I want you to understand as best you can what Scripture is teaching. But I want you to mix with these facts a full cup of discernment. The last thing I want to happen is that we become a body of strict, narrow-minded, exclusive people who have no room for folks who are not as "informed" as we. If in the process of reading the books in this study series you become less concerned about the person without Christ, something is missing. Consider it an alarm signal going off in your head. Life was never meant to be two-dimensional. It's multidimensional, because our God is full of beauty, color, variety, depth, and grace. Yes, always grace.

Root Issues

1. Gaining biblical knowledge seems to have at least two built-in dangers— the danger of pride and the danger of becoming rigid and narrow-minded. In what ways can you guard yourself against these twin spiritual hazards as you seek to grow in your knowledge of the truth?

2. Take another look at Paul's wholehearted prayer for the Philippian believers in Philippians 1:9-11. What does it mean to "love with discernment"? With your family? With fellow believers? Take time to think and pray through a situation in your own life where you might apply this truth.

3. From how many different sources are you drawing your spiritual nourishment? If you find that number is low, list in your notebook three to five additional sources that might help to balance your intake of truth. Your list could include books, booklets, radio broadcasts, tapes, church-sponsored Bible studies, or other sources that come to your

mind. Choose at least one from which you might begin receiving benefit this week. There is safety in a multitude of counselors!

Extending Your Roots

1. Write your first impression of the word *discernment*.

2. Compare your definition with a Bible dictionary meaning.

3. Combine your meaning and the dictionary meaning. *Discernment* means:

Taproot

1. Read Paul's prayer for the Philippian believers (Phil. 1:3-11) and write down his use of *discernment*.

2. Combine your meaning, the dictionary meaning, and Paul's meaning. *Discernment* means

Don't Forget to Add a Cup of Discernment

3. Think of one nondiscerning Christian that you know personally. How would you describe this person?

4. Does he or she seem to know the difference between right and wrong?

5. Does his or her church life seem out of balance with other Christians in your church?

6. The writer of Hebrews gives some positive advice on how to stay balanced as a Christian. Read Hebrews 5: 12-14.

7. Write a paragraph using the principles of discernment found in these verses.

8 Let's Start with a Few Definitions

Perhaps the best place to start is with several definitions . . . not dictionary definitions but practical, spiritually related definitions.

First of all, what do I mean when I talk about *knowledge*? By knowledge I mean an acquisition of biblical facts, principles, and doctrines. When I write about gaining knowledge, I have in mind an understanding of the great themes and principles of Scripture so that they fit together into a system of thought that assists us in accurately interpreting the whole of Scripture. Knowledge doesn't get emotionally involved. Knowledge alone lacks action. It lacks feelings. Knowledge has to do with the gaining, the gathering, and the relating of facts. And all of this can remain theoretical, if you let it.

Turn to 1 Corinthians, chapter 13. Let me show you a place where knowledge appears in this light. Interestingly, it occurs in a chapter on love.

> If I speak with the tongues of men and of angels, but do not have love, I have become a noisy gong or a clanging cymbal. And if I have the gift of prophecy, and know all mysteries and all knowledge; and if I have all faith, so as to remove mountains, but do not have love, I am nothing (vv. 1-2).

You remember these words. They begin the most wonderful treatise on love in all of literature. They cannot be improved upon. The reference to "knowledge" in these verses is a factual, doctrinal, theological, biblical kind of knowledge. But don't miss the emphasis: "Let there be love with knowledge!" Without love, all those facts leave us empty. "I am nothing."

Turn to 2 Corinthians, chapter 10. Same group of people—first-century Corinthians. Written a little bit later by the same writer, Paul. Second Corinthians 10:3-5 reads:

> For though we walk in the flesh, we do not war according to the flesh, for the weapons of our warfare are not of the flesh, but divinely powerful for the destruction of fortresses. We are destroying speculations and every lofty thing raised up against the *knowledge* [there's our word] of God, and we are taking every thought captive to the obedience of Christ .[emphasis mine].

The writer is referring to a knowledge of God, a knowledge about God, a knowledge of His Holy Word. Paul's point is well taken—such knowledge is often the target of our enemy's attack.

So much for knowledge. Next, what do I mean by *discernment*? This is the ability to detect, to recognize, to perceive beyond what is said. Now this may seem a little vague because it's not quite as exact and objective as knowledge. Discernment is the ability to "sense" by means of intuition. It is insight apart from the obvious, outside the realm of facts. People with discernment have the ability to read between the lines.

Think of being with a salesman who wants to sell you a car. In the process of listening to the person for a while, you sense in his presentation that he's not telling you the truth. Obviously, he doesn't have a three-by-five card sticking out of his upper pocket with bold print, reading, "I am a hypocrite. I do not tell the truth." But you say to yourself, "I don't trust this guy—something's not right." Why don't you trust him? Because you have perceived, you have *discerned* something that's either present or lacking in his words, or perhaps in his lack of eye contact or by the way he handles your questions.

Spiritually speaking, discernment enters into the realm of wisdom—the wisdom of God. Solomon specifically prayed for such wisdom. "So give Thy servant an understanding heart to judge Thy people to discern between good and evil" (1 Kings 3:9).

"I'm not asking You to make me rich," Solomon was saying. "I'm not asking You to make me famous. I'm not asking You to expand my territory. But I do ask You, O God, to give me discernment, to help me understand, to help me perceive beyond the realm of the visible and the audible."

Discernment includes the idea of sizing up a situation or a person correctly. Spotting evil that's lurking in the shadows. Sensing something that's missing. But it doesn't always have to do with matters of evil. Discernment also helps us sense truth and good. You discern when you are with certain individuals or listening to certain teachers that the person has character. Or that there is a lot of depth in that person's life. You detect that the person is presenting only a bit of what he or she really knows. You sense that there's a lot more behind the counter. Discernment signals such a message when we're with resourceful individuals.

In the second chapter of Proverbs we read about "discerning the fear of the Lord"(see v. 5). In the fourth chapter of 1 John it appears again—although not in those precise words: "Beloved, do not believe every spirit, but test the spirits to see whether they are from God; because many false prophets have gone out into the world" (v. 1). A lengthy paraphrase in today's terms might read: "Don't believe everything you hear. Put it to the test. Check it out. Mull it over. Talk it through. Think it out. Check it with Scripture. Be selective. Don't be gullible." Just because a man wears a collar doesn't mean he's to be considered "a godly man." Just because he speaks on radio or television or because he "seems so sincere" doesn't mean that he should be trusted and have your support. Just because he writes religious books or has charisma and presents his material in a persuasive, intriguing, interesting manner doesn't mean he is reputable. The New Testament commands us to test the spirits!

Look next at the first chapter of Philippians. It is verse 9 that interests me—Paul's prayer for the Philippians. "And this I pray, that your love may abound still more and more in real knowledge and all discernment."This is the only time in the New Testament that the noun "discernment" appears in the *New American Standard Bible*. The original Greek verb means "to perceive." He's praying, in effect, "That you may grow not only in complete knowledge, but in a broad range of perception."

I really wish I could describe to you how that happens, but I simply cannot. I don't believe there's a course you can take in some university on how to become more intuitive. Neither do I believe anyone can spell out the process in a step-by-step, one-two-three-four fashion. Discernment isn't taught as much as it's caught. But it can happen if you let it, if you seek it, if you spend time with those who model it.

Looking back at my earlier years once again, it's clear now that I didn't bother to cultivate discernment in my life. I was young. I was impressionable. I was caught up in the emotion, the momentum, the brilliance and persuasion of the teacher. I was swept into it along with hundreds of others. Maybe it is more accurate to say thousands. I silenced questions of doubt. I ignored a few inner reservations. Though in my heart I knew some things weren't right, I rationalized around them. I bought the whole package. My reservoir of knowledge was growing, but at the expense of my discernment.

Now, thank God, I'm growing in both. I wish I could dispense discernment to you in an easy-to-get fashion so that it could suddenly blossom in your life. I admit again, I cannot. Perhaps the warning is all that's needed to begin with. Be warned! Beware that if you drink at just one fountain, you will lose a great deal of the perspective that God wants to give you. It's like eating one food, or enjoying only one kind of entertainment, or reading only one author, or participating in only one exercise, or wearing only one color. How restrictive, how drab! Remember what Paul wrote: "I pray that you will grow in full knowledge and discernment."

There is a third term we need to define. I'm referring to *balance*. Although I haven't stated its importance, balance has been interwoven through most of this chapter. Frankly, it is a major objective of my life. What do I mean when I refer to balance? I have in mind remaining free of extremes, being able to see the whole picture—not just one side or a small part of it.

Maintaining one's spiritual equilibrium is another way to describe balance. Balanced Christians are realistic, tolerant people, patient with those who disagree. Serious when necessary, yet still having fun, still enjoying life. They are less and less intense, free from fanaticism. Furthermore, they are not afraid to say, "I don't know." They're still discovering. They listen to and value another opinion, even one with which they may disagree. They uphold the dignity of others, refusing to put them down. They are not easily threatened. Why? They're *balanced*! They realize they don't have all the truth. They're open to the possibility of alternative positions that give new slants and fresh perspective.

I read somewhere, many years ago, that heresy is nothing more than truth taken to an extreme. Check that out. Trace the heresies and you will find that they began with a certain truth that was pushed to an out-of-balance extreme.

Extending Your Roots

1. Sergeant Joe Friday of "Dragnet" fame used a phrase in every TV show that expressed his only interest in a criminal case, "just the facts please." What kind of attitude toward the Bible might a student develop if he receives only factual biblical instruction?

2. Listed below are some facts about Jesus Christ—just the facts. How can you gain wisdom and understanding using these facts?

3. Write down what eachfact means to you.
FACT: Jesus life, death, and resurrection fulfill in detail many Old Testament prophecies.

FACT: Jesus Christ is the unifying theme of the Bible—sixty-six books written by about forty authors thirteen hundred years ago in three original languages.

FACT: Jesus was born of a virgin.

FACT: The four Gospels agree in their harmonious portrayal of who Jesus is.

FACT: Jesus was worshiped as God and trusted as Savior by His early followers.

FACT: The letters of Paul were written and in circulation within twenty-five years after Jesus' death.

FACT: Jesus' discourses, parables, exhortations, and denunciations recorded in the Gospels are what we would expect from a divine-human person.

FACT: Jesus was entirely without sin.

FACT: Jesus was seen on more than a dozen occasions and by over five hundred people at once after His resurrection.

4. How can a student of the Bible acquire more than biblical information? Read Proverbs 1:7-9.

 *Taproot*

1. The Pharisees took a legalistic approach to life. They were *right* and *everyone* else was wrong. The following verses contain some information about legalism.

Read each verse and any cross-references by the verses. From these verses, list two things that are wrong with legalism.

Matthew 5:17-22
Matthew 12:10-12

1 Corinthians 10:25
Mark 2:21-22

2. Do you sometimes think being a Christian is the same as keeping a set of rules?

3. How does your life of freedom in Christ compare with a life of legalism?

9 | Some Examples from Scripture

In the Scriptures we find both positive and negative examples of this quality called "balance." The New Testament puts a red flag on individuals as well as churches where balance has gone out the window—instances where knowledge overshadows discernment. On the other hand, we find some examples where knowledge and discernment coexisted in beautiful balance.

Let's look at the negative examples before we focus on the positive.

Some Negative Examples

Tucked away in the obscure letter of 3 John is a classic example of one who lacked discernment. He has been called by some authors a first-century "church boss." A self-appointed authority. His name was Diotrephes. Here is a vivid pen portrait of an unbearable man. (There are a few in almost every church to this day. Rather than changing or softening in their older age, they simply remain unbearable.) Diotrephes is openly exposed and criticized by the apostle John in verses 9 and 10:

> I wrote something to the church; but Diotrephes, who loves to be first among them, does not accept what we say. For this reason, if I come, I will call attention to his deeds which he does, unjustly accusing us with wicked words; and not satisfied with this, neither does he himself receive the brethren, and he forbids those who desire to do so, and puts them out of the church.

In today's terms, the man was running the show. He became

a dangerous savage on the loose in a congregation. Apparently he was well-read and well-versed in the Old Testament Scripture. It is worth noting that there's not a word about his lacking knowledge. That could have been the reason he was brought to power and given leadership in the early church. But he became so overbearing in his leadership, so lacking in discernment (totally unaware that he was missing in tact, grace, and love) that John was forced to declare that Diotrephes was way out of line.

A lack of discernment is something like blindness. A crippling handicap. In the process of growing up in God's forever family, I plead with you to remain perceptive, gracious, and tolerant with others in the same family! Gain knowledge, certainly. But as you do, guard against becoming blinded by your own importance. Diotrephes failed at that very point. He lost his perspective. He lost his balance. He was in serious danger of bringing judgment upon himself.

The New Testament also cites a *church* that lacked discernment. The Corinthians—what a carnal corral of Christians! But don't misunderstand, those people were intellectually bright. They had lots of knowledge. They were open and extremely well taught. They knew their way around the block theologically. And they were cultured. The problem was that they couldn't get along with each other, which led to all kinds of difficulties. Their lack of spiritual equilibrium erupted into chaos. But before we get to that, look at a few verses in 1 Corinthians, chapter 1:

> I thank my God always concerning you, for the grace of God which was given you in Christ Jesus, that in everything you were enriched in Him, in all speech and all knowledge, even as the testimony concerning Christ was confirmed in you, so that you are not lacking in any gift (vv. 4-7).

What a place in which to worship during those early days! Talk about good teachers! And knowing the scoop! The Corinthians had a marvelous heritage. They had gained an understanding of the truth from Paul. Those truths were watered by Apollos, a gifted preacher, and nurtured by Christ.

That little isthmus in Greece contained a magnificent and exciting body of "with-it" people— the Corinthian church.

Ah, but look at verses 10 and 11. Those same people who possessed all that knowledge had made a royal mess of things.

> Now I exhort you, brethren, by the name of our Lord Jesus Christ, that you all agree, and there be no divisions among you, but you be made complete in the same mind and in the same judgment.
>
> For I have been informed concerning you, my brethren, by Chloe's people, that there are quarrels among you.

Quarrels? Among people with knowledge? Yes, quarrels. Because they weren't able to keep their knowledge in balance. They lacked the discernment to see what was happening. They missed the danger signals. As they grew in knowledge, they didn't grow in grace—a massive blind spot still found in churches today. They didn't perceive the dangers. They failed to add a cup of discernment to their bowl of knowledge.

Look a little further on in chapter 1, verse 12, for example.

> Now I mean this, that each one of you is saying, "I am of Paul," and "I of Apollos," and "I of Cephas," and "I of Christ."

There were cliques. One group followed the teachings of one individual to the exclusion of anyone else—first-century groupies who lived their so-called Christian lives out of balance. Not one but four distinct cliques. And obviously each of the four groups lacked discernment.

Chapter 3, verses 3 and 4:

> for you are still fleshly. For since there is jealousy and strife among you, are you not fleshly, and are you not walking like mere men?
>
> For when one says, "I am of Paul," and another, "I am of Apollos," are you not mere men?

What is Apollos ... and what is Paul? They're servants. Gifted men, but only men called by God to be spiritual leaders, not religious Pied Pipers.

Lest I overdraw the point, I'll restrain myself from going any further. But there is one thought I must underscore. You who are new in the Christian faith must constantly guard against getting all your food from one source. You need to vary your diet. You need to determine first if the teacher you are following is presenting biblical truth. But even if he or she is, you must always guard against believing it just because that one person says it—even if the person was the one who led you to Christ.

No one person has a corner on the truth. Never forget that!

And if you follow just one, you may very likely live to see the day you become disillusioned as that person reveals his or her feet of clay. I hope you will remember my warning for the rest of your life.

But later in the First Corinthian Letter we find these words:

> Now concerning things sacrificed to idols, we know that we all have knowledge. Knowledge makes arrogant, but love edifies. If any one supposes that he knows anything, he has not yet known as he ought to know (8:1-2).

Mark that well. If we think we've got it all together in knowledge, then, spiritually speaking, we hardly understand what knowledge is about. What is worse, such arrogance will cause us to lack dependence upon the Lord. And before the ink is dry on that warning, Paul goes on to describe the importance of restraining liberty for the sake of weaker brothers and sisters in the family of God who wouldn't understand.

Once again, please note it takes discernment to gauge one's actions. You don't simply gain a great deal of knowledge about liberty and then run wild with little concern about others. Your life-style speaks! A person with knowledge *and discernment* thinks about his life-style. Weighs his words and actions. Cares about others. That's all part of growing up in a balanced manner.

Some Positive Examples

Enough negatives! Let's look at a couple of positive examples. In the Book of Acts, chapter 18, we find a courageous, zealous young man named Apollos. At the end of that chapter we read of his ministry. Here was a bright, capable man, greatly gifted and wonderfully available. His theology, however, was a little thin at one point. And he listened to some people who knew more than he knew—an admirable trait!

> Now a certain Jew named Apollos, an Alexandrian by birth, an eloquent man, came to Ephesus; and he was mighty in the Scriptures (v. 24).

Did he know what he was talking about? You bet. Was he able to preach? With all his heart. Did anyone listen? Indeed. He was apparently quite an orator. In today's terms we'd say, "He had it together."

> This man had been instructed in the way of the Lord; and being fervent in spirit . . . (v. 25*a*).

"Fervent"? The word means "boiling"! So he was a passionate speaker. He had an electric, compelling delivery.

> he was speaking and teaching accurately the things concerning Jesus, being acquainted only with the baptism of John [so there were limitations in his knowledge]; and he began to speak out boldly in the synagogue. But when Priscilla and Aquila heard him . . . (vv. 25*b*-26*a*).

This was a husband-wife team who had been trained by Paul in Corinth, and later sent on to Ephesus to minister to a group of people there. Apollos traveled from Alexandria to Ephesus where the couple lived. He spoke openly of Christ. Aquila and Priscilla went to the meeting and heard him speak. As they listened, however, they *discerned* something was lacking. They must have loved his delivery. They, no doubt, appreciated his emphasis. But they realized he needed to know more. He didn't know about the ministry of the Holy Spirit. He only knew about salvation through Christ. He lacked a full knowledge of the truth. And perhaps they invited the young evangelist to come home with them that evening. Here's how it happened:

> and he began to speak out boldly in the synagogue. But when Priscilla and Aquila heard him, they took him aside and explained to him the way of God more accurately (v. 26b).

Apollos must have felt like a little puppy getting fresh food and water, encouragement, and love. He loved it! He was teachable. He discerned they knew what they were talking about. They discerned he needed to know more. So the discernment mixed with knowledge as the three of them met and melted together.

We're not told how much time they spent together—but apparently it was long enough to help Apollos develop what was missing in his theology. I am so impressed with his teachable spirit. Not many great preachers are open to the counsel of others. It's wonderful when you meet one who is willing to listen to another side, especially when he's willing to listen to others who point out what may be missing in his message.

After a period of time, Apollos was ready to leave.

> And when he wanted to go across to Achaia, the brethren encouraged him and wrote to the disciples to welcome him; and when he had arrived, he helped greatly those who had believed through grace (v. 27).

I would love to have heard Apollos, especially after his theology fell into place. Once he got that part of his theology honed to perfection he delivered the goods!

> for he powerfully refuted the Jews in public, demonstrating by the Scriptures that Jesus was the Christ (v. 28).

Because he mixed his knowledge with discernment, he was even better equipped. No one could refute him!

I don't care how gifted, how capable, how eloquent you may be, how widely used in your ministry; you can always benefit from the help of someone else—to hone, to sharpen you. Leadership requires accountability. You never get too old to be taught a new truth. Discernment says, "I know that my knowledge is limited. Others can help me. I am open and ready to learn."

Another example worth remembering is the church mentioned in chapter 17, verse 10 of the same book, the Book of Acts. The Berean church. This church had discernment.

> And the brethren immediately sent Paul and Silas away by night to Berea; and when they arrived, they went into the synagogue of the Jews.

And what about those people in Berea? Read very carefully:

> Now these were more noble-minded than those in Thessalonica, for they received the word with great eagerness, examining the Scriptures daily, to see whether these things were so (v. 11a).

What does it mean when we read they were "more noble-minded than those in Thessalonica"? Does that mean sophisticated? No. Were they closed, maybe suspicious? No. Everett Harrison writes:

> The nobility consisted in this, that instead of having a suspicious attitude which was ready to reject out of hand what was set before them they actually "received the word with great eagerness."[1]

There's a fine line between discernment and suspicion. These Bereans, when they heard the men who came to them with the truth, perked up, listened, and they remained open to what was presented. And did you notice what they did?

> for they received [the term means "welcomed"]—the word with great eagerness, examining the Scriptures daily, to see whether these things were so (v. 11b).

That's discernment. "Good truth, Paul! Great sermon, Silas! Man, they make a great dynamic duo. Those men can really preach. Now, let's go home and see if what they taught squares with the truth. Let's dig through the Scriptures and let's compare what they taught with what God's Word teaches. Let's make sure that that's really what we believe. We respect them. We know God has anointed them. His hand is certainly on their lives. But we don't believe it just because they said it. We believe it because it is in agreement with what God has written."

The Bereans added that necessary cup of discernment.

I certainly do not want to imply that all of us must become detectives, looking for clues of wrongdoing in another's life or teaching. It's one thing to be suspicious people who question everything we hear . . . and another thing entirely to be discerning, alert, perceptive. There is a very real need on our part every time we hear the Word proclaimed to listen closely, think it through, sift it out, compare it with other Scriptures and other material we've been taught.

Extending Your Roots

1. Use a concordance to locate all the Scripture references to discern or discernment in the Book of Proverbs. Write a dictionary-type definition for each meaning of the word.

2. What did you learn about discernment in your study?

3. Read about Diotrophes in 3 John. List four reasons why John denounced him as a church leader.

4. What can be done to help Christians confronting a similar situation?

Taproot

1. The Corinthian believers lacked discernment. Study 1 Corinthians to locate evidence of their blindness. What problems did the church have as a result?

2. Are these same problems found in your church?

3. What can *you* do to add a cup of discernment?

4. For a comparison read about the discerning church at Berea (Acts 17).

10 | Three Principles We Must Never Forget

Before wrapping up this part of our study, I want to mention three timeless principles. You may want to write them in the margin of your Bible alongside the comments we read about the church at Berea.

1. No one person has all the truth. Healthy Christians, young and old alike, maintain a variety in their diet. They draw truth from here and they draw it from there. They grow from this person and from that one—from this ministry and from that one. They realize there is not only wisdom but safety in a multitude of counselors.

2. No single church owns exclusive rights to your mind. Maybe I ought to broaden the word *church* to *ministry*. No single *ministry* owns exclusive rights to your thoughts. We are not to commit intellectual suicide when we become a part of any ministry. If we do, we're on our way to trouble. I think that might be the major reason God allowed a Jonestown. What a living memory in all our minds! So many of those sincere followers committed intellectual suicide as they absorbed and embraced only one man's message simply because he said it. In subtle ways he stole their allegiance, which belonged to Christ. Our submission is ultimately to one Head—the Lord Jesus Christ. We bow to the lordship of Christ, not the headship of some minister. To respect human leaders is commendable, but to follow them, *regardless*, is to flirt with danger.

3. No specific interpretation is correct just because a gifted teacher says so. If the Bereans felt Paul and Silas were worth comparing with Scripture, surely that says something about teachers and preachers today.

Well, there you have it. I really want you to live a fuller life than you now live, especially those of you who have settled for tunnel vision, lacking imagination. In fact, I don't want you to wind up your Christian life as I started mine, sacrificing the beauty and color, perception and creativity. For that reason I want to close this chapter with a story you'll never forget.

There were once two men, both seriously ill, in the same small room of a great hospital. Quite a small room, just large enough for the pair of them—two beds, two bedside lockers, a door opening on the hall, and one window looking out on the world.

One of the men, as part of his treatment, was allowed to sit up in bed for an hour in the afternoon (something that had to do with draining the fluid from his lungs), and his bed was next to the window.

But the other man had to spend all his time flat on his back—and both of them had to be kept quiet and still. Which was the reason they were in the small room by themselves, and they were grateful for peace and privacy—none of the bustle and clatter and prying eyes of the general ward for them.

Of course, one of the disadvantages of their condition was that they weren't allowed much to do: no reading, no radio, certainly no television—they just had to keep quiet and still, just the two of them.

They used to talk for hours and hours—about their wives, their children, their homes, their former jobs, their hobbies, their childhood, what they did during the war, where they had been on vacations—all that sort of thing. Every afternoon, when the man in the bed next to the window was propped up for his hour, he would pass the time by describing what he could see outside. And the other man began to live for those hours.

The window apparently overlooked a park with a lake where there were ducks and swans, children throwing them bread and sailing model boats, and young lovers walking hand in hand beneath the trees. And there were flowers and stretches of grass and games of softball, people taking their ease in the sunshine, and right at the back, behind the fringe of the trees, a fine view of the city skyline.

The man on his back would listen to all of this, enjoying every minute—how a child nearly fell into the lake, how beautiful the girls were in their summer dresses, and then an exciting ball game, or a boy playing with his puppy. It got to the place that he could almost see what was happening outside.

Then one fine afternoon, when there was some sort of parade, the thought struck him: Why should the man next to the window have all the pleasure of seeing what was going on? Why shouldn't he get the chance?

He felt ashamed and tried not to think like that, but the more he tried, the worse he wanted to change. He'd do anything!

In a few days he had turned sour. He should be by the window. And he brooded and couldn't sleep, and grew even more seriously ill—which none of the doctors understood.

One night, as he stared at the ceiling, the other man (the man next to the window) suddenly woke up coughing and choking, the fluid congesting in his lungs, his hands groping for the button that would bring the night nurse running. But the man watched without moving.

The coughing racked the darkness—on and on—choked off—then stopped. The sound of breathing stopped—and the man continued to stare at the ceiling.

In the morning, the day nurse came in with water for their baths and found the other man dead. They took away his body, quietly, no fuss.

As soon as it seemed decent, the man asked if he could be moved to the bed next to the window. And they moved him, tucked him in, and made him quite comfortable, and left him alone to be quiet and still.

The minute they'd gone, he propped himself up on one elbow, painfully and laboriously, and looked out the window. It faced a blank wall.[1]

As I said earlier, for several years my life faced a blank wall, I lacked any imagination. Life was comprised of blacks and whites—neatly boxed, tightly sealed. I was very little help to anyone else.

Today, your life may literally face a blank wall, and the only thing you can draw on is the beauty and depth and color prompted by God's Book. You need more than knowledge, you need a new infusion of creativity from the Spirit of God Himself. In a word, you need discernment.

Don't miss it. Add a full cup of it to your knowledge. Mix it well, and you'll never lose your balance.

Extending Your Roots

1. Read Paul's prayer for the Philippians (1:9-11). On your blank wall write your prayer to God about your discernment needs. Pause right here and pray.

Taproot

1. Read again the story of the two men. If you had been next to the window, what would you describe related to God's Word?

Part
III

The Bible

11 God's Book—
God's Voice

What is your final authority in life?

I mean, when you're cornered, when you're really up against it, when you're forced to face reality, upon what do you lean?

Before you answer too quickly, think about it for a few moments. When it comes to establishing a standard for morality, what's your ruler? When you need an ethical compass to find your way out of an ethical jungle, where's north? When you're on a stormy, churning sea of emotions, which lighthouse shows you where to find the shore?

Let me get even more specific. While getting dressed one morning you notice a dark mole on your side, just above your waist. A few days later you observe that it is surrounded by red, sensitive flesh. It's becoming increasingly more sensitive to touch. You're disturbed about it. You finally talk yourself into seeing a physician. The surgeon probes and pushes, asks some pertinent questions, takes a few x-rays, and finally says to you with a frown, "I don't like the way this looks. And I don't like the way it feels. I'll have to remove it—we'll do a biopsy." You churn inside while he talks. After the procedure he pays a visit to your room and tells you that his report isn't good. In fact, he quietly informs you, "It is melanoma." The worst kind of cancer. How do you handle that? To whom or to what do you turn? You need something solid to lean on. What is it?

Here's another: It's between one and two o'clock early one morning when your phone rings. It's a police officer. He tries to be tactful, but it's obvious that someone you love very much has been in an automobile accident—a terrible head-on collision. The victim—your loved one—suffered a tragic death. He tells you he has the unenviable and unfortunate responsibility of asking you to come and identify the body. What do you do in the hours that follow? How do you handle your grief? What gives you the courage to accept the truth—to go on?

Here's another: You've worked very, very hard in your own business. Your diligence has been marked by integrity, loyalty, sacrifice. You've given up a lot of personal desires and comforts so that the business might grow. You've plowed what little bit of profit you've made right back into the operation. And you've never once compromised your principles. But during the last few hours you've discovered that your product, which has taken the best years of your life to perfect, will soon be obsolete, thanks to a recent technological breakthrough. In fact, it appears that within the next few months you may lose everything. The awful reality of financial bankruptcy suddenly looms like a massive shadow. Where do you turn? How do you stay on your feet?

Just one more: You've been married a little over twenty-five years. You and your partner have reared three now-adult children. One will soon finish college, and the other two are gone, both happily married. You're thinking that the future will soon reward you with relief and relaxation. You have been faithful to your mate. You've worked hard and you've given yourself to this marriage. Out of the blue one evening your partner sits down beside you and begins by saying, "I . . . can't keep something from you any longer. There's someone else in my life. In fact, I don't want to be married anymore. I . . . I don't love you. I don't want to be in this home anymore. I want out of the marriage. I'm divorcing you." What gives you the stability you need to continue your life? How do you keep from becoming bitter? Where do you turn to find hope amidst such rejection?

I've worked with people for more than twenty-five years. And I've seen them in the worst kind of crises. I've seen some who could not take it. They ultimately took their lives, and I buried them. I've seen others who lost their minds. Some lost their will to go on. Others became physically ill or attempted to dodge the reality of the pain through drugs or alcohol abuse. I've visited with them and tried to help them through it. In the chapters that follow, we'll look at some ways people have of facing life's crises. Then we'll explore the firm foundation available to those who rely on God's Word.

Root Issues

1. Does the Bible serve as a shelter for you when the storms rage in your life? It's no good to try and construct a shelter *after* the storm descends, you need one ready *before* the winds begin to howl. Take some time to identify at least five "shelter" verses from Scripture—promises of God's unfailing love and sustaining power. (Your pastor or a mature Christian friend might enjoy helping you locate these verses if you're not sure where to start.) Ask your spouse or a friend to hold you accountable to memorize those verses in a reasonable length of time.

2. That's all! Carefully evaluate your activities over the past week. What portion of your time and energies were devoted to either personally interacting with biblical truth or building that truth into the lives of others? What small (but significant) steps could you take over this coming week to move that percentage toward eternal priorities? Remember to capture these insights in your notebook.

3. How long has it been since you've joined with another person—or perhaps a small group—to work through a Bible study together? If you're uninvolved, consider scheduling a weekly time with one or more believers to search through a portion of God's Word together. Ask the folks at your local Christian bookstore for help in selecting some material suited to your needs.

4. How can you guard against "biblical abuse" as you

teach others—or even as you represent God and Scripture in casual conversation? If you realize that you have been using Scripture in a "proof text" manner, determine right now to *always* study the context so that you will *maintain the meaning*.

5. If the Bible you use is full of notes and comments from an unreliable source, perhaps you need to purchase another Bible. By starting over with clean, unmarked pages, you will be able to construct a fresh path to the truth.

6. Commit to memory the "what, who, why, where, and when" statements you'll read in chapter 18. Review them until they are fixed in your mind. Remind yourself of them each time you study the Scriptures.

 *Extending Your Roots*

1. Write your definition of authority. Use a dictionary to verify the meaning.

12 Common Crutches People Lean On

It has been my observation through the years that people usually do one of four things when they are faced with crises. I think of these responses as common crutches on which people lean. The first I would call, for lack of a better title, *escapism*. Most people, at least initially, escape the reality of the pain. They run. They either run away emotionally or they literally run in physical ways through travel, affairs, or chemical dependence. They deny the horror of what has happened. They refuse to let reality run its course and take its toll on them. They escape.

Second, I've noticed many people turn to *cynicism*. They not only face their troubles, they become preoccupied with them. And they grow dark within. Surprise leads to disillusionment. And they let that fester into resentment and finally bitterness. Often they spend the balance of their lives trying to take revenge. They become victims of their own lack of forgiveness. They begin to live out the message on the bumper sticker: "I don't get mad . . . I get even." Whether their hostility is directed toward God, or some other person, they turn to cynicism. More often than not, the cynic ships the faith as bitterness wins the final victory.

Third, there is the crutch of *humanism*. They listen to the counsel of some other person rather than God. They get their logic and their reasoning from a man, a woman, or a book. They turn to self-help, people's opinion, self-realization. They try human reasoning, which inevitably is based on horizontal human wisdom. And it leaves them empty, it leaves them lacking. Or they try meditation, which fails to satisfy. And they do not really come to terms with the truth of what they could learn through the whole experience.

Fourth, the crutch of *supernaturalism*. This may be mild or maddening. Some people turn to mediums. They seek information from the other world. They get in touch with witches and wizards with the assurance of demonic powers. Some begin to try astrology and others turn to superstition. More and more connect with the occult as they are trying to cope with their world of pain.

Popular though these four crutches may be, escapism, cynicism, humanism, and supernaturalism do not provide any sense of ultimate relief and satisfaction. They leave the victim in quicksand—more desperately confused than at the beginning. None of the above is an acceptable "final authority."

So I return to the question that opened the preceding chapter: What is your final authority in life? What holds you together when your life falls apart?

There can be no more reliable authority on earth than God's Word, the Bible. This timeless, trustworthy source of truth holds the key that unlocks life's mysteries. It alone provides us with the shelter we need in times of storm.

Extending Your Roots

1. The Bible offers many examples of people who used the crutches of *escapism, cynicism, humanism,* or *supernaturalism*.

Read the following Scripture passages and identify the person or groups involved. Decide which response they chose to their "quicksand." Describe the crutch on which they chose to lean.

Genesis 13:12-13 _____

Genesis 39:10-18 _____

1 Samuel 20:30-33 _____

1 Kings 18:19 _____

Common Crutches People Lean On

Acts 8:9-11 _____

2 Timothy 4:10 _____

Jonah 1:3 _____

Luke 12:17-19 _____

1 Kings 19:3-4 _____

Acts 17:19-21 _____

2. The final authority on earth is God's Word—the source of truth. Locate in the Gospels at least three times Jesus used the word *truth*.

3. Complete this sentence: My final authority in life is

4. Explain your answer.

 *Taproot*

1. The reliability of Bible truth has always been under attack. Peter gave a defense of biblical authority. Outline Peter's claim to the authority of Scripture from 2 Peter 1:16-21.

13 | The Bible: The Absolutely Trustworthy Crutch

If I could have only one wish for God's people, it would be that all of us would return to the Word of God, that we would realize once for all that His Book has the answers. The Bible *is* the authority, the final resting place of our cares, our worries, our griefs, our tragedies, our sorrows, and our surprises. It is the final answer to our questions, our search. Turning back to the Scriptures will provide something that nothing else on the entire earth will provide.

Psalm 119 speaks of a man who knows what it means to hurt. He needs help outside himself. The specifics may be different from what I've described thus far, but he is no stranger to suffering. He's going through hard times. He says,

> My soul languishes for Thy salvation;
> I wait for Thy word (v. 81).

In other words, "I wait for the truth of Your Word to come to pass, Lord. I wait for help to return. I wait for the promises to become a reality. I wait for the wisdom to take shape and to make sense in my life." That's what the psalmist means when he writes, "I wait for Your Word." Notice he waits for God's Word, not human reasoning, not his own feelings, and not for a chance to get even.

Let's read on:

> My eyes fail with longing for Thy word,
> While I say, "When wilt Thou comfort Me?" (v. 82).

God's assistance is not always immediate. He doesn't

come swiftly every time we cry out for help. Most Christians I know are currently "longing for Thy word" to bring needed relief in at least one major area of life. Read verses 85-87:

> The arrogant have dug pits for me,
> Men who are not in accord with Thy law.
> All Thy commandments are faithful;
> They have persecuted me with a lie; help me!
> [Here is a man being criticized. He's under the gun.]
> They almost destroyed me on earth,
> But as for me, I did not forsake Thy precepts.
> ["I come back to Thy word, O God."]

Then verses 89 and 90:

> Forever, O Lord,
> Thy word is settled in heaven.
> Thy faithfulness continues throughout all
> generations.

And finally, verse 92. I love it!

> If Thy law had not been my delight,
> Then I would have perished in my affliction.

Isn't that the truth! If I hadn't had the eternal foundation of the Book of God on many an occasion, my very life would have been finished.

In a world of relativism, the Bible talks in terms of right and wrong, good and bad, yes and no, true and false. In a world where we're encouraged to do it "if it feels good," the Bible addresses what is sinful and what is holy. Scripture never leaves us with a bewildered look on our faces, wondering about the issues of life. It says, "This is the way it is. That is the way it is not to be. This is the way to walk; do not walk there." It tells us straight. It provides the kind of solid foundation you and I need.

Why the Foundation Is So Dependable

But wait. We need to understand why. Why is it that this Book qualifies as our final authority?

Its Identity

First, I think it will help us to know something about the identity of the Bible. By the way, the term *Bible* is never once found in Scripture. It's not a biblical term. So what does the Bible call itself? What is its identity?

Let's take a look into the Gospel by Luke, chapter 24. Jesus is speaking with two men on the road to Emmaus. In verse 27 we read of the outcome of that historic walk together:

> And beginning with Moses and with all the prophets, He explained to them the things concerning Himself in all the Scriptures.

Jesus verbally worked His way through the Old Testament, called here "the Scriptures." A little later on, the two men related to their friends what had happened:

> And they said to one another, "Were not our hearts burning within us while He was speaking to us on the road, while He was explaining the Scriptures to us?" (v. 32).

Again, they referred to "the Scriptures." Very interesting term, "Scriptures." It is a translation of the Greek term *graphe*. (We get our word *graph* from it.) It means "that which is written." In other words, the sacred writings. When we rely on the Bible, we rely on that which has been *written*. I linger here because I think it's significant that God didn't simply *think* His message. He didn't simply *speak* His message or reveal it in the clouds or through dreams to men and women in biblical times. No, He saw to it that His Word was actually written down. He put it in the language of the people so that people in all generations could read it and grasp its significance. He "graphed" His Word. We're grateful we have a book that contains the very mind of our God—the Scriptures—in written form.

Moving from Luke's Gospel let's look next at the seventeenth chapter of John. This entire chapter is a prayer. It's the longest recorded prayer of the Lord Jesus Christ in all the Bible. While praying He says to the Father:

The Bible: The Absolutely Trustworthy Crutch

I have given them Thy word; and the world has hated them, because they are not of the world, even as I am not of the world. I do not ask Thee to take them out of the world, but to keep them from the evil one. They are not of the world, even as I am not of the world. Sanctify them in the truth; Thy word is truth (vv. 14-17).

I am so grateful those verses are in the Bible. Look again at that closing comment. What an absolute statement from the lips of Jesus! "Thy Word is truth." In four monosyllabic words we find the basis of our belief in the veracity, the reliability of Scripture. This is not human counsel, it is truth—divine counsel. It is honest. It has integrity. It is as absolute as it is timeless. "Your Word, O God, is truth."

I appreciate what James Montgomery Boice once wrote regarding the relevance of this claim:

> We talk about the Word of God as truth. We are right to do so. But we have to acknowledge when we speak along those lines that the world of our day no longer strictly believes in truth. The great apologists of our time are all saying that. C. S. Lewis said it very well in the opening pages of *The Screwtape Letters,* where the devil's henchman, tempting his patient on earth, is advised not to talk about truth and falsehood because people don't operate on that basis anymore, but rather to talk about what's useful or what's practical. "That's the way to get through," says the devil.
>
> Francis Schaeffer has said the same thing in more philosophical terms. He's pointed out quite rightly that today, unlike previous generations, people, though they speak of truth and falsehood, are not speaking of truth in the biblical sense or even in the traditional sense to mean that which is true now and will always be true universally. Rather they mean that which is true now but not necessarily tomorrow or yesterday; or it is true for me but not necessarily for you. In other words, truth for contemporary men and women is relative.
>
> But here we have truth embodied in the Scriptures. . . .
>
> Here the efficacy of the Word of God comes in: the fact that God really uses the Word to accomplish his purposes,

whether men and women believe in the Word of truth or not.[1]

Talk about a familiar line of logic! We've heard such reasoning, haven't we? "A thinking person shouldn't cut off his head when he starts getting serious about religion. There are lots of things out there that we have to consider . . . lots of stuff beyond the bounds of this Book." Certainly, there are. But truth, real truth, truth you can rely on, truth that will never turn sour, that will never backfire, that's the truth in this Book. That's what this Book is about. That's why this Book provides us with *the* constant and *the* needed crutch.

By the way, do *you* turn to it for the truth you need? The longer I live the more I realize that most people on this earth have an amazing ability to twist truth—to change things so that right isn't really right, it's partially right. And wrong isn't really wrong, it's sort of unfortunate—somewhere between OK and I'm not really sure. The world system talks about truth, but it doesn't ever identify it. I have to make up my mind with my own moral standard or my own ethical compass. I'm left to choose the direction I want to go. And no one is going to lay any trip on me, because nobody else knows where the boundaries are. And therefore I am left not free—definitely not free—but quasi-paralyzed between bewilderment and confusion. That, my friend, is bondage!

What does it take to free us? It takes truth. Yes, the truth. It was Jesus Himself who once promised, "You shall know the truth and the truth shall make you free" (John 8:32).

I was born in 1934. I have now lived nearly sixty years—long enough to realize that I desperately need truth in my life. I've been exposed to just enough human intelligence to be dangerous! I've gotten just enough of man's wisdom not to trust in it. I don't need more of those things in my life. I need truth. I need God's "yes" and God's "no," God's light and God's mind. That explains why I appreciate the Scripture so much. His Word provides the truth I need. It erases the doubts, it gives a sure footing even though I am surrounded by people in a swamp of uncertainty.

It's interesting that in all of my research for this book, I did not find one source that God made much of the next verse I want us to look at. And it's surprising, because it's one of the most helpful on this subject. I'm referring to 1 Thessalonians, chapter 2, verse 13 that the Scripture is "God's message." That it is, in fact, "God's Word."

> And for this reason we also constantly thank God that when you received from us the word of God's message, you accepted it not as the word of men, but for what it really is, the word of God, which also performs its work in you who believe.

"When I stood to speak," Paul is saying, "and I delivered to you God's message and I unrolled the scrolls and pointed out the truth of what Moses had written and what Jeremiah had said and what Amos had pointed out—when I presented that to you, you didn't take that as the word of man. You saw it for what it really was—the very word of God."

Frankly, that does something to you. When you realize that the print on the page you are reading is, in fact, God's message, God's Word, it stands alone. Absolutely unique—in a class by itself. Think of it this way: God's Book is, as it were, God's voice. If our Lord were to make Himself visible and return to earth and speak His message, it would be in keeping with this Book. His message of truth would tie in exactly with what you see in Scripture. His opinion, His counsel, His commands, His desires, His warnings, His very mind. When you rely on God's voice, God's very message, you have a sure foundation.

Now one more thought regarding identity—and it's the practical side of the subject. Let's look at 1 Peter, chapter 1, verses 22-25. Referring to the same writings, the same truth, the same message of God, Peter writes:

> Since you have in obedience to the truth purified your souls for a sincere love of the brethren, fervently love one another from the heart, for you have been born again not of

seed which is perishable but imperishable, that is, through the living and abiding word of God. For,
"All flesh is like grass,
And all its glory like the flower of grass.
The grass withers,
And the flower falls off,
But the word of the Lord abides forever."
And this is the word which was preached to you.

Here is another reference to the everlasting nature of God's message.

Do you realize there are only two eternal things on earth today? Only two: people and God's Word. Everything else will ultimately be burned up—*everything* else. Kind of sets your priorities straight, doesn't it?

I smile understandingly at the story that Charlie "Tremendous" Jones tells about walking down into his basement after the Youngstown flood had left its damage. As the water receded and left thick mud and gunk almost waist deep, he walked into his basement where he had displayed all of his awards and all of his plaques and all of his honors, now under four feet of mud. His response went something like this: "I stood there, staring in disbelief as I heard the voice of God. He said, 'Charlie "Not-So-Tremendous" Jones, don't worry about all this, I was gonna burn it all up anyway!' "

The stuff we place on the shelf, the things we put frames around, the trophies and whatnots we shine and want to show off, the things we're so proud of—it's all headed for the final bonfire. But not God's Book! Peter reminds us that the truth will "abide forever." Grass will come, it will flower . . . and then it will wither and die. But His written message, the truth, will abide forever.

Its Inerrancy

But wait. How can anyone get so excited about something that was written by men? We have no problem with the Giver of truth. He gave it, but wasn't the truth corrupted when He relayed it to earth through the hands of sinful men?

This is the perfect moment for you to become acquainted with three doctrinal terms you need to remember. It wouldn't hurt for you to commit them to memory: revelation, inspiration, and illumination. *Revelation* occurred when God gave His truth. *Inspiration* occurred when the writers of Scripture received and recorded His truth. Today, when we understand and apply His truth, that's *illumination*. That would include discovering new truth for our lives, understanding it, and implementing it.

Revelation has ceased. Inspiration has ceased. But illumination is going on right up to this moment!

Isn't that a great thought? Right now as you hold this book in your hands and as you grasp what I am writing regarding Scripture, the Holy Spirit is incessantly at work instructing you and affirming your thoughts and giving you new hope and clear direction.

Now then, thinking back over those three terms, you realize that the most critical of the three is inspiration.

In the same way, the critical point of your confidence in the Bible is directly related to your confidence in its inspiration. How then can we be sure that God's Word is free from error and therefore deserving of our trust?

There is great help in 2 Timothy, chapter 3. (We visited with Timothy earlier in this book.) You'll recall that Timothy has just been exhorted to maintain his godly priorities regardless of the times in which he lived—days which were marked by difficulty and depravity and deception (vv. 1-13).

Then these words appear:

> You, however, continue in the things you have learned and become convinced of, knowing from whom you have learned them; and that from the childhood you have known the sacred writings [*graphe*, there's our word again for sacred writings] which are able to give you the wisdom that leads to salvation through faith which is in Christ Jesus. All Scripture is inspired by God and profitable for teaching, for reproof, for correction, for training in righteousness (vv. 14-16).

Having said that about the Scriptures, Paul verifies His confidence in inerrancy, "Timothy, all *graphe,* all the writings of God, all Scripture is 'inspired of God.' " If you use the *New International Version* of Scripture, you see it as literally as we can render it in English: "God-breathed." When God revealed His truth for human writers to record, He "breathed out" His Word. It says in verse 16 that all Scripture is inspired because it has been miraculously "God-breathed." Not inspired like a Picasso, not inspired like a sculpture by Michelangelo, not inspired like a great composition by Handel or Brahms, not inspired like a literary masterwork by Shakespeare, but inspired, as in "God-*breathed.*" All Scripture has been "breathed out" by God.

Now, wait a minute. This still doesn't fully answer your question, does it?

When I breathe out my message to my secretary, she takes it and she writes it down and goes back over it with me and then types it and gives it to me so I can sign the letter. The process is called taking dictation. Did the writers of Scripture take dictation?

If you know much about the Bible, you realize that it includes different personalities. Peter doesn't sound a lot like John. And John doesn't sound like David. And David's writings aren't like Paul's. And Paul is altogether distinct from Jude or Peter or, for that matter, any of the other apostles. So somehow there was the preservation of each writer's personality without corrupting the text. That rules out the idea of dictation. So we have a Bible full of human personality and style, and yet it's God who breathed out His message. And it came in written form from the pens of men who differed in style.

Then how did He do it? How did He make that happen? Second Peter 1, verses 19-21:

> And so we have the prophetic word made more sure, to which you do well to pay attention as to a lamp shining in a dark place, until the day dawns and the morning star arises in your hearts. But know this first of all, that no prophecy of

> Scripture is a matter of one's own interpretation, for no prophecy was ever made by an act of human will.

Let me interrupt. Paul didn't sit down one day and think, "Let's see, I think I'll write 2 Corinthians." Or, "I feel like Galatians. I'll write Galatians today." No prophecy ever came to pass because of the impulse or the inner urging of the will of man. No, in contrast to that, the key word in verse 21b is *moved.*

> but men moved by the Holy Spirit spoke from God.

This English word *moved* is translated from an ancient Greek nautical term. In extrabiblical literature it was used to describe ships at sea. When a ship had lost its sails and its rudder, and it was at the mercy of the winds and the waves and the currents of the sea, it moved along apart from its own power. It remained a ship, but it was without its own power and energy. That's the word used here, not referring to ships at sea but writers of Scripture. They were moved outside their own power and energy as they wrote His truth.

So what we have is the preservation of an inerrant text. God breathed out His message to human writers, who, without losing their own style and personality, wrote His truth under His divine control. And because He superintended the process in its entirety, no error was present right down to the very words of the original text. What Scripture says, God says—through human agents, without error.

I appreciate professor Paul Feinberg's insightful comment:

> Inerrancy means that when all facts are known, the Scriptures in their original autographs and properly interpreted will be shown to be wholly true in everything that they affirm, whether that has to do with doctrine or morality or with the social, physical, or life sciences.[2]

Can I rely on it? Is it reliable when I go through those experiences I wrote about in chapter 11? Absolutely and unreservedly.

Its Reliability

We started in Psalm 119. Let's end in the same chapter. Interwoven through this magnificent psalm is one theme, "I rely on Your word, O God." God has established His precepts, and the psalmist again and again declares their reliability. He's given us a morality to follow. He helps us with our greed, with ethics, with integrity, with verbal attacks from others, feeling lonely, and on and on. We could read right through this psalm, and we would uncover most of life's major battles. Each time the writer returns to the same throbbing theme and says, "I rely on Your Word . . . I find Your Word dependable . . . I realize it has never once failed me."

And it is still true today. Amazing, isn't it? This ancient, inerrant Book is reliable right up into these closing days of the twentieth century. I like what an old Baptist scholar named A. T. Robertson once wrote with tongue in cheek, "One proof of the inspiration of Scripture is that it has withstood so many years of poor preaching." It's remarkable that this Book is still around after the way some of us have been handling it, sometimes *mishandling* it. I'll say more about that in chapter 15.

 *Extending Your Roots*

1. Read through Psalm 119 and circle all the words that refer to the Scripture. Focus on verse 92. Does the Bible provide the solid foundation you need to face the realities of life? Explain your answer.

2. Define what the Bible is and its place in your life using the contrast of *is* and *is not*.

The Bible is   *The Bible is not*

14 Benefits of Relying on the Bible

In Psalm 119:98-100, we find three wonderful benefits of relying on the Bible. What benefits come my way when I rely on this marvelous Book?

Stability

Thy commandments make me wiser than my enemies, for they are ever mine (v. 98).

First benefit: *stability* in the midst of storm. I realize you have not been immune to stormy times in your life. No doubt you bear the marks and the scars, the hurt and the pain in your face. And if you could see me, you'd see them in mine. That's part of being in the human race. But the wonderful thing about relying on God's Book is that it gives you stability. It gives you that deep sense of purpose and meaning, even when you get the phone call in the middle of the night, even when your mate says, "It's over," even when, for some unrevealed reason, bankruptcy comes unexpectedly and leaves you financially vulnerable. No other counsel will get you through in the long haul like the stability that comes from God's Book.

Insight

I have more insight than all my teachers, for Thy testimonies are my meditation (v. 99).

Here's a second benefit: *insight.* Students love verse 99! But it doesn't mean you can pull rank on your prof (I'd not suggest that you try that.) It says you will have *insight* rather than *intimidation*. There are few scenes more intimidating than the scholarly world. But the interesting twist to that is this—people who really know their Bibles aren't intimidated. Scholarly arguments designed to paint Scripture in a poor light don't pin you to the mat. Nor can you be battered in such a way because you realize that what they are saying isn't really truth—it's a misuse of Scripture. But I've observed when people really get a knowledge of the Scriptures and they begin to rely on that knowledge and see it work in their lives, they are less and less threatened by such attacks. They can face criticism, important people, and strong words, and even be outnumbered in an educational scene, but not be intimidated because they have the truth which gives them insight, the ability to see beyond the obvious.

By the way, the Bible will always be under attack in secular schools of higher learning. One scholar explains why.

> Satan does not waste his ammunition. Professors, who are being paid to teach philosophy, English, biology . . . mathematics, often take time from their class periods to undermine the Bible and orthodox Christianity. Why are they not doing the same with the sacred books of other religions? The answer is that Satan, the original liar, is sympathetic with books that lie. His real enmity is directed against the book of truth because it contains the dynamite for his defeat.[1]

Maturity

> I understand more than the aged,
> because I have observed Thy precepts (v. 100).

We gain *maturity* beyond our years by relying on Scripture. I don't meet too many people who say, "I'm very satisfied with my level of maturity." Most people I talk to say, "I'd love to grow up. I'd love to be stronger in my faith. I'd love to learn from the dumb mistakes I have made and not keep making them . . . I'd love to be mature." The hope for such maturity is in God's Word. You will have "understanding more than the aged" as you rely on this Book.

I wrestle with a basic question: How do I close a chapter as full as this one? Perhaps with this one thought: It is the simple truth that holds you together in the most complex situations. Not simplistic, but simple. The profound truth that the Bible gives us is like a warm blanket wrapped around us on a cold night.

Let me conclude with three quick questions: Do you want stability? Would you like insight? Is it your desire to have maturity? Of course! Absolutely. All that—and so much more—can be found in God's reliable Word. Even if you have spent most of your years questioning God's authority, wondering about God's Book, question and wonder no longer.

Return to this taproot of truth. Lean on it. Start today. It will hold you up and keep you strong. When it comes to a "final authority" in life, the Bible measures up.

 *Extending Your Roots*

1. The word *Bible* is not a biblical term. What words are used to identify *the* Book?

Read and record the terms:.

John 20:9	Romans 15:4
Psalm 12:6	Luke 4:21
Isaiah 5:24	2 Timothy 2:15

2. God has a message for you. In 2 Timothy 3:16, Paul says two things about Scripture. They are ＿＿＿＿＿ and ＿＿＿＿＿＿＿＿＿＿＿ .

3. Explain the idea of "God-breathed" as used in 2

Timothy 3:14-16 (NIV). God breathed out His message to human writers. Listed below are some of God's writers. Record beside their names what they wrote.

David   Solomon
Paul   Samuel

4. What human writers did God use to present His message in:
- The Ten Commandments
- The birth of Jesus
- The Sermon on the Mount
- The "faith" chapter (Heb. 11)
- The book on eschatology

5. According to Psalms 119:98-100, three benefits are available to the believer who depends on God's Word.
(1) stability
(2) insight
(3) maturity
For a better understanding of these benefits, complete the following assignments:
Stability. Jonah experienced a literal storm of nature and a storm of spirit. Analyze both storms and record what happened in each. How could Jonah have found stability?

 *Taproot*

Insight. Read verse 99. Consider the experience of the apostle Paul before the Athenian philosophers as recorded in Acts 17: 16-34. What an intimidating situation! Or was it?

Outline the Acts passage with an emphasis on Paul's benefit of insight into the Scripture.

Maturity. In a paragraph, state the outcome of the mature and immature builders recorded in Matthew 7:24-29. What primary lesson was Jesus teaching concerning His Word?

1. Read the following promises. After each Scripture reference, write a personal situation or "battle" to which this promise could apply.

Romans 8:38-39
John 14:12-14
Matthew 7:7-11
Mark 8:34-35

2. Why is the Bible our "final authority"?

3. God's Word works. Do you agree or disagree? Explain.

Read for affirmation:
- Isaiah 34:16
- 2 Corinthians 1:13-14
- 1 Timothy 1:15
- Isaiah 40:38

4. Write a summary paragraph entitled: "How I view the authority of the Bible."

15 Handling the Scriptures Accurately

Life has many disappointments. But I doubt if there is one any greater than the realization that you have been abused. Webster defines abuse as ". . . a deceitful act . . . a corrupt practice or custom, improper use or treatment."

Ours is a day of abuse: sexual abuse, emotional abuse, verbal abuse. But what about *biblical* abuse? By that I mean being deceived by the improper use of Scripture. Who of us has not witnessed someone twisting Scripture, forcing it to mean something it does not mean? Those who don't know better start believing it with all their heart, only to discover later on that both the interpretation and the application were fallacious, perhaps dangerous to their spiritual health and growth.

We hear about all kinds of abuse in this generation, but seldom do we hear from victims of biblical abuse, though they number into the thousands. In my opinion, it is one of the major problems among Christians today. I think it's not an exaggeration to call it "the ultimate rip-off." Can you imagine the disillusionment following the realization that the information you were given, which you believed to be true, was in fact erroneous—the result of gross mishandling of Scripture?

The Problem: Mishandling the Bible

Now this has nothing to do with *sincerity*. Many, perhaps most, people who mishandle the Word are very sincere. And it really has little to do with *theology*. Some who have their theology fairly well in place can still mishandle Scripture. It also has nothing to do with *personality*. There are gifted teachers dripping with charisma who can sway an audience and hold them in the palm of their hand, yet be guilty of mishandling Scripture. It certainly has nothing to do with *popularity*. Famous, highly visible personalities in Christian circles who draw large listening audiences can (and often *do)* mishandle Scripture. So let's put to bed, once for all, the idea that if a person just "loves the Lord," he or she will be preserved from mishandling Scripture. No, even those of us who believe in the inerrancy of Scripture and affirm the importance of sound doctrine can be guilty of biblical abuse.

Most likely there are problems of Scripture abuse unique to each country. Our problem in America is not the availability of Scripture. We have numerous copies of the Bible. I looked on the shelf in my study the other day and counted sixteen Bibles! Among them were about twelve different versions or paraphrases of the Scriptures in various sizes, print styles, and with a selection of study notes from reputable scholars. And that doesn't include those in my home. There are probably several copies of the Scriptures in your home as well.

No, our problem in this country is not a lack of Bibles; it is a lack of people who carefully handle the Word of God, both privately and publicly. I'm convinced that we should not simply be students of the Scriptures—sound in our theology—but that we must also be careful in our interpretation of the Scriptures. And the more we teach, the greater that need!

This is nothing new. You will find the problem of biblical abuse mentioned often in the New Testament. It may not have been called that, but it went on, nevertheless.

 *Extending Your Roots*

1. Have you ever thought about how words differ in the Christian and non-Christian vocabularies? Notice what

Jesus was doing when He talked to Nicodemus. Read John 3:1-21. Jesus was translating words into Nicodemus' language.

Try changing the following words. Translate each Bible word from the Christian meaning to what the non-Christian *thinks* you mean.

WORD	CHRISTIAN	NON-CHRISTIAN
repent		
accept Jesus		
into		
your heart		
believe		
everlasting life		
born again		
pray		
Savior		
Lord		
filled		
hope		
heaven		
other:		

2. Decide whether the statements below are *biblical abuse* or *biblical truth* statements. Place a *BA* in the space before biblical abuse and *BT* before biblical truth statements.

_____ Sin is not real (1 John 1:6,8).

_____ Jesus was not the Messiah.

_____ Jesus was human—only.

_____ Christians can do whatever they like without fear of judgment (Jude 4).

_____ How I live has little to do with my faith (Jude 4).

_____ God doesn't sentence people to hell (Jude 7).

_____ The gift of God is eternal life.

_____ All people have sinned.

Growing Deep in the Christian Life: The Bible

 *Taproot*

1. Write a dialogue with someone, similar to that of Jesus and Nicodemus, as a way to practice using right words.

2. Based on the biblical abuse statements above, describe the life-style of a Christian who believes these errors.

16 Our Need: Maintaining the Meaning

On several occasions in the New Testament, people are mentioned who failed to maintain the meaning of Scripture. And in each case they were people who knew better. Are you ready for a surprise? Many of them were professional clergymen—the scribes and the Pharisees—people in the first century who took the Scriptures seriously. They were not theological liberals, nor were they people who were soft on divine revelation. On the contrary, they devoted their lives to the Scripture, but they mishandled it.

Look first at Matthew 9:10-12:

> And it happened that as He was reclining at the table in the house, behold many tax-gatherers and sinners came and were dining with Jesus and His disciples. And when the Pharisees saw this, they said to His disciples, "Why is your Teacher eating with the tax-gatherers and sinners?" But when He heard this, He said, "It is not those who are healthy who need a physician, but those who are sick."

Didn't Jesus have a marvelous way of addressing the real issue? With incredible insight He never failed to cut through all the fog. But now the point. In verse 13 He quotes Hosea, chapter 6, to the Pharisees:

> But go and learn what this means, "I desire compassion, and not sacrifice," for I did not come to call the righteous, but sinners.

Notice the veiled rebuke. It was as if He said, "Go and learn the meaning of the verse you know by heart!: 'I desire compassion, and not sacrifice.'" I'm sure they had taught that verse from the prophet Hosea, along with many other related passages. I'm sure they had it neatly tucked away in their hearts. Yet they didn't even know the meaning of it! So, He said, in effect, "Go and learn what it means, men!"

Next, take a look at Matthew 12. We'll see a similar situation. As you read this account, notice Jesus' question, "Have you not read?"

> At that time Jesus went on the Sabbath through the grainfields, and His disciples became hungry and began to pick the heads of grain and eat. But when the Pharisees saw it, they said to Him, "Behold, Your disciples do what is not lawful to do on a Sabbath." But He said to them, "Have you not read what David did, when he became hungry, he and his companions; how he entered the house of God, and they ate the consecrated bread, which was not lawful for him to eat, nor for those with him, but for the priests alone? Or have you not read in the Law, that on the Sabbath the priests in the temple break the Sabbath, and are innocent? But I say to you, that something greater than the temple is here. But if you had known what this means, 'I desire compassion, and not a sacrifice,' you would not have condemned the innocent. For the Son of Man is Lord of the Sabbath" (vv. 1-8).

Look back and underscore Jesus' exhortation: "If you had known what this means, . . . you would not have condemned the innocent." Strange words! An extremely reliable New Testament scholar observes:

> Our Lord does not deny that rest on the Sabbath is commanded, and He does not stay to protest against the rigor which would make plucking and eating corn a violation of the command. He points out that every rule has its limitations, and that ceremonial regulations must yield to the higher claims of charity and necessity.[1]

But they hadn't thought that through. They had learned a line from the scroll. They had, no doubt, committed it to memory. And then they went about the business of looking for people who were breaking the letter of the law. Pharisees and scribes were notorious for omitting the spirit of the law. Because they missed the deep meaning of the passage of Scripture, because they failed to handle it wisely, they committed biblical abuse. And that is precisely what goes on today by well-meaning, sincere people. May we never forget Jesus' observation, "If you had known what this means, . . . you would not have condemned the innocent."

Look next into Matthew, chapter 15. The intensity increases:

> Then some Pharisees and scribes came to Jesus from Jerusalem, saying, "Why do Your disciples transgress the tradition of the elders? For they do not wash their hands when they eat bread." And He answered and said to them, "And why do you yourselves transgress the commandment of God for the sake of your tradition? For God said, 'Honor your father and mother,' and 'He who speaks evil of father or mother, let him be put to death.' But you say, 'Whoever shall say to his father or mother, "Anything of mine you might have been helped by has been given to God," he is not to honor his father or his mother.' And thus you invalidated the word of God for the sake of your tradition. You hypocrites, rightly did Isaiah prophesy of you, saying,
>> 'This people honors Me with their lips,
>> But their heart is far away from Me.
>> But in vain do they worship Me.
>> Teaching as doctrines the
>> precepts of men.' "

And after He called the multitude to Him, He said to them, "Hear and understand. Not what enters into the mouth defiles the man, but what proceeds out of the mouth, this defiles the man" (vv. 1-11).

Talk about severe! "The Scripture says, 'Honor your father and mother,' but you have taken the very lines of Scripture and you have twisted them so that they fit what you want them to say. And I'm calling your hand on it," implies our Lord. Don't miss His pointed rebuke: "You invalidated what the [Scripture says] for the sake of your tradition." And then He calls them hypocrites!

I love the statement made by His disciples:

> Then the disciples came and said to Him, "Do You know that the Pharisees were offended when they heard this statement?" (v. 12).

Isn't that great? "Do you realize You made them angry?" I doubt very seriously that Jesus ever lost much sleep over making people like that angry.

> But He answered and said, "Every plant which My heavenly Father did not plant shall be rooted up. Let them alone; they are blind guides of the blind [wow!]. And if a blind man guides a blind man, both will fall into a pit" (vv. 13-14).

Strong counsel! I enjoy reading these verses to folks who mistakenly think of Jesus as a wimp—sort of a human doormat. On the contrary! Don't miss what our Lord felt so strongly about. He despised the way those hypocrites mishandled the Word. In effect, He said, "They have My Book, and they're making it say something it was never meant to say."

Maybe you don't need such a warning, but perhaps someone you know does. Just because a person opens the Scripture and calls himself or herself a teacher of the Bible doesn't guarantee the message. Just because they are well-known, just because people hang on their every word, just because they have great followings, and just because they travel the world over, carrying a Bible and teaching from the Bible, none of that guarantees they're right. Be careful about people who lift lines from the Scriptures and adapt them to what they want those passages to say. Scribes and Pharisees live on today. Their problem? They may quote Scripture correctly, but they fail to maintain the correct meaning of God's Word.

Now, sometimes it's the hearer's fault. And that is a completely different problem. In Matthew, chapter 16, we find a case in point. Jesus didn't mishandle the Scripture; those who heard Him misinterpreted what He said. Read verses 5-7:

> And the disciples came to the other side and had forgotten
> to take bread. And Jesus said to them, "Watch out and be-
> ware of the leaven of the Pharisees and Sadducees." And
> they began to discuss among themselves, saying, "It is be-
> cause we took no bread."

Note: That's not at all what Jesus meant. They misunder-
stood Him. Keep reading:

> But Jesus, aware of this, said, "You men of little faith, why
> do you discuss among yourselves that you have no bread? Do
> you not yet understand or remember the five loaves of the
> five thousand, and how many baskets you took up? Or the
> seven loaves of the four thousand, and how many large bas-
> kets you took up? How is it that you do not understand that I
> did not speak to you concerning bread? But beware of the
> leaven of the Pharisees and Sadducees" (vv. 8-11).

Then it "clicked." It took them a while, but they finally put
the pieces of the puzzle together.

> Then they understood that He did not say to beware of the
> leaven of bread, but of the teaching of the Pharisees and Sad-
> ducees (v. 12).

Now the reason I linger over this is because the same
thing occurs today. Sometimes teachers and preachers work
extremely hard to speak the truth from Scripture and to
maintain its meaning. There are occasions when Scripture
is a bit symbolic. And there are hearers who take things so
directly, so literally, that they miss the meaning behind the
symbol—the significance of what the passage is teaching,
even though the teacher tries to keep that from happening.
Hearers (like the disciples) either miss it altogether or they
twist part of it so that the meaning becomes confused. The
disciples said He was talking about literal bread. He was
talking about the leaven (a symbol of evil) of the Pharisees.
Let's not forget our goal: It is always to MAINTAIN THE
MEANING OF SCRIPTURE.

May I pass along one of the major secrets of accomplishing that goal? When you study or when you teach or when

you hear, pay attention to words. Now you might be thinking, *How elementary can you get? Of course you pay attention to words.* No, a lot of people don't. A lot of people speak in vague paragraphs. They roll together a lot of thoughts and ideas like kneading dough. And you have to dig through it to figure out what's there. But the best teachers, like the best students, are ever conscious of words.

One of the best things I've ever read on handling the Scriptures with accuracy came from an article written by Dr. Bernard Ramm. In this fine piece he talks about being sensitive to words.

> The good interpreter never looks at a word without a question mark in his mind. He may consult his Greek lexicon, or his Webster's, or a commentary, or a concordance. But he fusses around among his books till the word upon which he has fixed his attention begins to glow with meaning.
>
> An experienced doctor has a wonderful sensitivity in his fingers. He has spent a lifetime feeling lumps, swellings, growths, tumors, and wens. He knows their textures, their shapes, and their peculiarities. Where our fingers tell us two things, a doctor's fingers might tell him a dozen things. Just as a doctor's fingers have a feel for lumps and growths, so a Bible teacher must have a feel for words. He must pass the fingers of his mind over their shapes, textures, and peculiarities.
>
> This means sensitivity to phrases, clauses, paragraphs, and idioms. A good Bible teacher is restless; he takes nothing for granted. He is the detective whose victim is the meaning and the words in their various combinations of phrases, sentences, and paragraphs are the clues. Out of the various configurations of the words he delves for the meaning. He looks for the train of thought (i.e., the sequence in meaning) and tries to follow it throughout the passage. He works, digs, meditates, ruminates, and studies until the meaning of the biblical text shines through.
>
> It is right at this point where the poor teacher fails. He is content with his efforts even though his thoughts are vague and his impressions are indistinct. As soon as he gets a good exhortation or practical application, he's content and rests

at that point. He does not sit with a restless mind and dig and sweat, until he has achieved the meaning of the text.[2]

When you study the Bible, always pay close attention to words. Never miss the significant ones. Pull out your dictionary; trace the meaning of key words. Talk the words through; think the words through. Compare that word with another word and another place in Scripture where a similar word is used so that you will begin to see the meaning of the passage. John R. W. Stott refers to the importance of concentrating on words like a dog worrying over a bone.

 *Extending Your Roots*

1. Misinterpretation of the Scriptures is a serious thing to do. Read 2 Peter 3:15-16. Summarize the verses below.

2. God does not confuse us by hiding Himself and His truth. Read Psalm 119:130. Put this verse in your own words.

Definition: Biblical interpretation is discovering what the writer is trying to say, communicating that meaning to others, and applying the passage to life.

Certain principles must be followed for responsible interpretation.

(1) Set the passage in the proper context. (Caution: Don't lift verses out of context.)

(2) Consider the background.

(3) Determine the meaning of biblical words and phrases.

3. Now, apply these principles to Psalm 51. Recall the situation of King David's sin.

4. Discover how confession of sin brings about renewal.

5. Explain why you need to be personally responsible for your sins.

6. How can you use the example of David's sin and Psalm 51 to help a person restore the joy of salvation?

The study of the principles of interpreting the Bible is called hermeneutics. Purchase from a Christian bookstore a book about interpreting the Bible.

Use these questions for practice interpretation.

1. Jesus gave specific directions to the seventy messengers in Luke 10:1-12. Which directions apply only to that setting? Which directions apply to spreading the gospel today?

2. Read Luke 14:26. What do you think Jesus means when He said that a person who comes after Him must hate his own father and mother?

17 An Example: Ezra and the Scroll

Dr. Ramm's advice from the last chapter is vividly illustrated in the Old Testament Book of Nehemiah, chapter 8. Here is one of the clearest examples in all of the Scriptures where the Bible was handled accurately, where its words, their meaning, and overall application were correctly rendered for the people. Here is biblical exposition at its best.

Before I point out four observations from this passage as it relates to Ezra and the scroll, let's allow Scripture to set the stage.

> And all the people gathered as one man at the square which was in front of the Water Gate, and they asked Ezra the scribe to bring the book of the law of Moses which the Lord had given to Israel. Then Ezra the priest brought the law before the assembly of men, women, and all who could listen with understanding, on the first day of the seventh month. And he read from it before the square which was in front of the Water Gate from early morning until midday, in the presence of men and women, those who could understand; and all the people were attentive to the book of the law. And Ezra the scribe stood at a wooden podium [this is the first place in all the Bible where even a passing reference is made to a pulpit] which they had made for the purpose (vv. 1-4).

Got the picture? Lots of people. A priest named Ezra. The scroll of God—an ancient copy of the Hebrew Scripture. A pulpit. Great interest in what God's Word had to say. So much for the background. Now for the four observations, each having to do with the careful manner in which God's Word was handled. No abuse here!

First: *Accurately handling the Scriptures starts with the reading of Scripture.* You will observe that Ezra read from the book of the law, and that those who listened "were attentive to the book of the law" (v. 3). And in verse 5:

> [He] opened the book in the sight of all the people for he was standing above all the people . . .

Now the reason I emphasize that is because I want you to notice that the focus was upon the Book of God, not some performer, not some program that they came to applaud, not even the opinion and wisdom of this man Ezra, though he was certainly a wise, godly, greatly respected man.

When reading from the Book of God, it is terribly important that everyone realize its importance. And if we're going to handle the Book of God accurately, then the Scripture must form the basis of our thoughts—not someone's idea, not the teacher's lesson plan, not even a preacher's opinion. Let Scripture speak for itself! And that's what those people focused on when they heard the Scriptures read. That's what they gave attention to. First, there must be the reading of Scripture.

> and when he opened it, all the people stood up (v. 5).

Second: *Accurately handling the Scriptures includes having respect for the Scriptures.* This needs to be underscored again and again. They were attentive to the book, and when Ezra opened the book in their sight, all the people stood up. Those things illustrate respect. Furthermore, there was a podium, which seems to emphasize an attitude of authority. They showed reverence when they stood, and as they listened "from early morning until midday." And verse 6 tells us of their submissive response:

> Then Ezra blessed the Lord the great God. And all the people answered, "Amen, Amen!" while lifting up their hands; then they bowed low and worshiped the Lord with their faces to the ground.

This isn't just casual listening (like planning the menu for the week while the Scripture is being presented). This is focused attention and full concentration upon the Book of God. What an awesome sight it must have been!

For the next few moments I invite you to come into my study with me. When I begin to prepare a biblical message, a sermon, or a scriptural talk, I begin not with *Time* or *Newsweek* magazine, not with the newspaper, not with someone's comment that was made to me, not even some book about the Bible. Nor do I start with an event I saw on television or something I've read on an airplane that week (as important as those things may be for illustration). My first place of reference is the open Bible. What does it actually say?

I often read the passage aloud. I read it repeatedly. I read it with emphasis and feeling. I pause. I think. I take some time to pray over that section. I think it through as best I can until it becomes very familiar in my mind. I read it over and over and over again so that the focus of my concentration is upon Scripture. I become so familiar with it that I can "see" it in my mind without having to look at it all the time.

I am occasionally surprised to meet men in the ministry who don't do that. They come to a passage with a bias or with an idea of something they want to say, and they start looking for a verse that says it for them. And it's amazing— they'll find it! That's called "proof texting." You can prove anything (yes, anything!) you want to prove from Scripture if you just stop reading soon enough and don't finish the thought, or if you twist a term here and there, "spiritualizing" the meaning. Or if you start in the middle of a paragraph and don't consider the context, you can make it say what you want it to say. And every time you do, you abuse! But those who refuse to commit biblical abuse don't go about it that way.

As we've already noticed, that's certainly not what Ezra did. He said to the people, as it were, "Let's hear from God. Let's unroll the scroll." And they stood to their feet. And he read from the law of God. And they said, without any comment from him, "Amen, Amen! We believe it. That's the Book. That's the truth. We care about what God says." But he didn't stop there. When God's Book was opened, it was as if God were speaking.

Third: *Accurately handling the Scriptures means that the truth is explained so that all can understand.* Now I'm glad to say, we've come to one of the clearest verses on biblical exposition in all the Old Testament.

> And they read from the book, from the law of God, translating to give the sense so that they understood the reading (v. 8).

Go back to those words and find the term "translating." Don't go any further. Let's be like a dog and worry over this bone for a few moments. The original term meant "to make distinct, to separate." An acceptable paraphrase: "to take apart for the sake of making something clear and understandable so that the truth would fall in place."

But why was there a need to translate? Stop and think. Who were those people? They were Hebrews. In what language was the scroll written? In Hebrew. But where had the people been? According to Jewish history, they'd been in captivity for seven decades. Some of them didn't know what life was like *outside* captivity. They had been born in captivity and lived their entire lives among the Babylonians. Their whole frame of reference was Babylonian or Chaldean. Their language was Chaldean. They thought in Chaldean. Their culture, their life-style was Chaldean— but the Book of God was written in Hebrew. Not only were they removed from the truth by centuries since its writing, they were removed from the truth culturally and linguistically. All the more reason to "to translate to make distinct."

In other words, when Ezra and his scribes built the bridge of understanding in the minds of the people, they took the Hebrew Scriptures and made them distinct to a Chaldean mind. That is always the job of the Bible teacher—building a linguistic and cultural bridge from Scripture's original setting to today's audience.

Today we are even further removed from the days of the Bible. So the Scripture is not only nineteen centuries old, it's from another continent. It's also from another culture. The careful student of Scripture will keep that uppermost in mind.

Please observe next, they gave "the sense." They translated "to give the *sense.*" The original term means "insight, to see into something." They shed light on that which was otherwise unclear to the listener. And the result? The people understood the reading.

For many years I have believed that the greatest test of good biblical communication occurs a day or two after people have heard what is taught . . . when they can sit down at their kitchen table and go back through that passage—and can pretty well explain what it meant in that day and how it applies today.

Now for the fourth and final observation: *Accurately handling the Scriptures results in obedience to the Scriptures.* Bible study, like any theoretical knowledge, is not an end in itself. It is a means to an end. Accurately handling the Scriptures results in specific, personal acts of obedience to the Scriptures. Let's watch that happen! Take your time and read through these verses:

> Then Nehemiah, who was the governor, and Ezra the priest and scribe, and the Levites who taught the people said to all the people, "This day is holy to the Lord your God; do not mourn or weep." For all the people were weeping when they heard the words of the law. Then he said to them, "Go, eat of the fat, drink of the sweet, and send portions to him who has nothing prepared; for this day is holy to our Lord. Do not be grieved, for the joy of the Lord is your strength." So the Levites calmed all the people, saying, "Be still, for the day is holy, do not be grieved." And all the people went away to eat, to drink, to send portions and to celebrate a great festival, because they understood the words which had been made known to them.

Then on the second day the heads of fathers' households of all the people, the priests, and the Levites were gathered to Ezra the scribe that they might gain insight into the words of the law. And they found written in the law how the Lord had commanded through Moses that the sons of Israel should live in booths during the feast of the seventh month. So they proclaimed and circulated a proclamation in all their cities and in Jerusalem, saying, "Go out to the hills, and bring olive branches, and wild olive branches, myrtle branches, palm branches, and branches of other leafy trees, to make booths, as it is written." So the people went out and brought them and made booths for themselves, each on his roof, and in their courts, and in the courts of the house of God, and in the square at the Water Gate, and in the square at the Gate of Ephraim. And the entire assembly of those who had returned from the captivity made booths and lived in them. The sons of Israel had indeed not done so from the days of Joshua the son of Nun to that day. And there was great rejoicing. And he read from the book of the law of God daily, from the first day to the last day. And they celebrated the feast seven days, and on the eighth day there was a solemn assembly according to the ordinance (vv. 9-18).

They heard what God said and they did it. Rather plain and simple, huh? But that's obedience—doing what God says.

Allow me to return one more time to Bernard Ramm's comments:

I feel that I have experienced a good session of Bible study:
- when I felt the teacher took me right into the text and not around it.
- when I felt we interacted with the text itself and not with the party-line beliefs of the teacher. [You've had that experience, haven't you?]
- when I felt that I had a better understanding of the text than when I came into the session.
- when I felt that the time was basically spent in meanings and not in a miscellany of religious platitudes.
- when I felt challenged, comforted, encouraged, and practically instructed.[1]

Extending Your Roots

1. Accurately handing the Scriptures results in specific, personal acts of obedience to the Scriptures.

But what happens when people do not follow God's instructions? Read the following examples and complete the chart.

People	God's Instruction	Disobedience	Result
Adam and Eve	Genesis 2		
Moses	Numbers 20		
King Saul	1 Samuel 15		

2. Complete this sentence: Handling the Scriptures accurately means that I must

Taproot

1. Little is known about the prophet Ezekiel's life. However, throughout his book, his acts of obedience to God's instructions are evident. Write what God instructed and how Ezekiel obeyed.

2:1 _____

3:24-27 _____

4:1ff. _____

5:1-4 _____

12:2-7 _____

21:2 _____

24:16-17 _____

18 Tools for the Trade

Some of you are getting downright serious about Bible study. Good for you! Since that is true, you need to get hold of some tools that will help you do that. I call these tools abuse busters!

First, you need a *Bible concordance,* which is an alphabetical listing of all the words in the Bible. The bigger the concordance, the more the words. Some are exhaustive, meaning they include every word that appears on every page of the Bible. No serious student of the Scriptures should be without a copy of a reputable concordance.

Second, you need a *Bible dictionary.* Like an English dictionary, this book defines and describes the major terms, places, and people in Scripture. Numerous dictionaries are available. Take your choice. Talk to your local Christian bookstore and have the manager show you the options.

Third, you need a *Bible atlas* which gives you maps and helpful geographical observations of the world in biblical days.

Fourth, you need some *Bible commentaries.* Initially, you need to have one that covers the whole of Scripture in one volume. Then you should begin to purchase individual commentaries on the individual books in the Bible. Serious Bible students get serious about purchasing biblical tools. Be forewarned: They're not 98-cent booklets. So don't drop by a store with $1.50, planning to buy two or three of them!

Tools for the Trade

Warning for the Wise

In chapter 15, I referred to being biblically abused. One of the interesting (albeit tragic) facts of child abuse in our day is the fact that most parents who abuse their children were themselves abused. I find the same is true of scriptural abuse. My warning? People who were abused biblically tend to abuse others biblically. If you happened to have been abused, how about breaking the trend? Just face the fact that you were ripped off. And rather than sending hate mail to your teacher of yesteryear and wasting hours of valuable time resenting what you were taught, just commit yourself to change. Forgive him or her and pay no more attention to those old teachings. Get away from the former error and commit yourself to God's Word afresh and anew. Set up a reading program so that you can begin to absorb the Scripture. Begin to build a new respect for the Bible. Use helpful tools as you seek a clear, careful understanding, ultimately living obediently in keeping with God's Word.

Some Principles to Remember

Want some help on breaking the old syndrome? How about five simple rules? Each includes a different word—what, who, why, where, and when.

1. WHAT. *Never forget what you are handling.* And what is that? It is the Word of God. God's Book—God's voice. That will keep you *sensitive.*

2. WHO. *Always remember who has the authority.* That's the Lord Himself. That'll keep you *humble.* I was speaking with some Christians recently, and they commented on a particular Bible teacher they had heard. The thing that disturbed them the most about this person was an air of arrogance. Nothing was wrong with his competence, his theology, or his years of experience. But there was an unattractive arrogance about his style. Confidence is essential, but proud arrogance has no place whatsoever in Bible teaching. When I hear an arrogant teacher, I realize I'm listening to a person who has forgotten who has the authority.

Those who remember who has the authority don't have a big battle with pride.

3. WHY. *Keep in mind why you are teaching.* This will keep you *accurate.* Why study? Why teach? To capture the original meaning and then today's application of the Scriptures. Would it help if I drilled it home with a couple of "nots" or negatives?

First, your desire is not to impress. Don't try to "wow" others with your scholarship. If you've got it, they will notice it and be impressed on their own. No reason to toss in Hebrew or Greek words unless they really help clarify the subject. If it doesn't really help your case, forget the original language barrage. If it does, refer to it sparingly. It confuses an English audience to parade a lot of Greek or Hebrew verbiage in front of them in rapid-fire fashion.

Second, try not to ride a hobbyhorse. Now I realize everybody has a few. I've got 'em, you've got 'em. Sometimes I get on 'em, I confess. But when I do I realize later that I rode away from my point rather than toward it.

Try to remember those two negatives as you keep in mind why you are teaching. Accuracy is always the underlying goal of Bible study and Bible teaching.

4. WHERE. *Think about where people are.* That'll keep you *interesting.* If you're dealing with people in southern California, it takes one kind of approach. If you're dealing with people in the Northeast, it takes another kind of approach. The Deep South calls for yet another. If you're dealing with folks on the mission field, yet another kind of approach is best. Or with prisoners, another. If you're dealing with folk in a situation where there's very little knowledge of Scripture, your presentation will be more interesting if you'll remember where they are. They're not as far along as others in another circle. To keep it interesting remember where.

5. WHEN. *Focus on when the teaching ends.* That'll keep you *practical.* When the teaching is all over, when the Bible study that you've been involved in is history, what difference will it make?

I never intended this discussion to be so long . . . but the deeper I got into the subject, the more I felt needed to be said. After all, there are few things more important than handling the Scriptures accurately.

Those who are committed to these principles, those who put them into action, will become part of the solution to biblical abuse.

Extending Your Roots

Match the following Bible study tools with the correct description.

1. _____Bible commentary

2. _____Bible dictionary

3. _____A theological wordbook

4. _____Bible encyclopedia

5. _____Bible concordance

6. _____Bible atlas

a. Helps us find Scripture references if we know only a word or phrase from the verse.

b. A multivolume detailed, scholarly work to help us with a more exhaustive treatment of various subjects.

c. Provides detailed information about words, persons, places, and events.

d. Helps us locate key places in the Bible

e. Provides an introduction to each book of the Bible and some help in interpreting the book's contents.

f. Explains the meanings, uses, and applications of various biblical terms, including the root meaning of the terms.

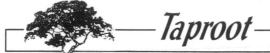
Taproot

See what you can find out about 2 Peter 1:12-21 if you use some of the Bible study tools.

1. A good title for this passage:

2. Author (from a Bible dictionary):

3. Time of writing (from a commentary):

4. Theme of the book (from a commentary or dictionary):

5. Word and phrase study (a theological wordbook, concordance, and various translations of the Bible ie. NIV)

v. 13. "tent of this body"

v. 16. "eyewitness of his majesty"

v. 17. "Majestic Glory"

v. 18. "the sacred mountain"

v. 19. "prophets" "morning star"

v. 20. "interpretation"

v. 21. "will of man"

6. From this study I have come to better understand

Five simple principles are presented about handling the Scriptures accurately. Under each important rule, write a summary paragraph about how you will be committed to these principles.

1. WHAT: Never forget what you are handling.

2. WHO: Always remember who has the authority.

3. WHY: Keep in mind why are are teaching.

4. WHERE: Think about where people are.

5. WHEN: Focus on when the teaching ends.

Consider these questions. When the teaching and Bible study are over in your Sunday School class this week, what difference will it make? What evidence of learning will you see Monday? Keep a one-week record of how your life was changed when the Bible teaching ended.

Notes

Part I

Chapter 1

1. Jaime O'Neill, "No Allusions in the Classroom," *Newsweek,* 30 September 1985.

Chapter 5

1. *Newsweek,* 30 September 1985, 22.

Chapter 6

1. C. S. Lewis, "Learning in Wartime," *The Weight of Glory and Other Addresses* (New York: Macmillan Co., 1949), 50-51.

Chapter 9

1. Everett F. Harrison, *Acts: The Expanding Church* (Chicago: Moody Press, 1975), 264.

Chapter 10

1. G.W. Target, "The Window" from *The Window and Other Essays* (Boise, ID: Pacific Press Publishing Association, 1973), 5-7.

Part II

Chapter 13

1. James M. Boice, "The Marks of the Church," *Can We Trust the Bible?* ed. Earl D. Radmacher (Wheaton, IL: Tyndale House, 1979), 80-81.
2. Paul Feinberg, "The Meaning of Inerrancy," *Inerrancy,* ed. Norman Geisler (Grand Rapids, MI: Zondervan, 1980), 294.

Chapter 14

1. Roy Aldrich, "The Wisdom of the Word," *Bibliotheca Sacra* 124 (April-June 1967): 61.

Chapter 16

1. Alfred Plummer, *An Exegetical Commentary on the Gospel According to St. Matthew* (Grand Rapids, MI: Wm. B. Eerdmans, 1960), 172.

Chapter 16

1. Bernard Ramm, "But It Isn't Bible Study," *Eternity Magazine,* February 1960, 3.
2. Ibid., 4

Chapter 17

1. Bernard Ramm, "But It Isn't Bible Study," *Eternity Magazine,* February 1960.